Captivated Health®

TAKE CONTROL.
GAIN TRANSPARENCY.
LEVERAGE CONFIDENCE.

Other Books by the Author

Bend the Healthcare Trend (2009 and 2017): How Consumer-Driven Health and Wellness Plans Lower Insurance Costs

Inspire to Act (2014): Short Stories that Touch Your Heart, Enrich Your Soul and Inspire You to Act

Captivated Health

TAKE CONTROL.
GAIN TRANSPARENCY.
LEVERAGE CONFIDENCE.

A Platform to Transform Your Health
Insurance Plan from an Expense into an Asset

MARK S. GAUNYA, GBA

ethos
collective

Printed in the United States of America

Published by Igniting Souls
PO Box 43, Powell, OH 43065
IgnitingSouls.com

LCCN: 2025911816

Paperback ISBN: 978-1-63680-537-5
Hardback ISBN: 978-1-63680-538-2
eBook ISBN: 978-1-63680-539-9

Available in paperback, hardcover, e-book, and audiobook.

Any Internet addresses (websites, blogs, etc.) and telephone numbers printed in this book are offered as a resource. They are not intended in any way to be or imply an endorsement by Igniting Souls, nor does Igniting Souls vouch for the content of these sites and numbers for the life of this book.

Some names and identifying details may have been changed to protect the privacy of individuals.

The superscript symbol IP listed throughout this book is known as the unique certification mark created and owned by Instant IP[IP]. Its use signifies that the corresponding expression (words, phrases, chart, graph, etc.) has been protected by Instant IP[IP] via smart contract. Instant IP[IP] is designed with the patented smart contract solution (US Patent: 11,928,748), which creates an immutable time-stamped first layer and fast layer identifying the moment in time an idea is filed on the blockchain. This solution can be used in defending intellectual property protection. Infringing upon the respective intellectual property, i.e., IP, is subject to and punishable in a court of law.

Dedication

I dedicate this book to the executive leaders of the thousands of middle-market employers who provide health insurance to fifty million Americans and invest over $500 billion per year in their health and well-being. And to the employees and their families who are the healthcare consumers who use those health insurance benefits. You all deserve a healthcare system that is built for you, not for the rule-making players who designed it. You deserve transparency of quality and price and informed, caring support as you navigate your healthcare journey. You deserve a set of principles that become the new foundation for an outcomes-based, higher-quality, less expensive health insurance system that makes healthcare easier and more affordable.

It's time to reject the "less bad renewal" and get off the hamster wheel[IP] by taking control, gaining transparency, and leveraging your confidence to create a better healthcare future, transforming your health insurance expense into an asset.

Table of Contents

Foreword

IT WAS OVER a decade ago when I met Mark Gaunya while attending and speaking at a captive self-insurance conference. There are those moments when you encounter someone and know right away—whether it be because of a shared vision or passion—that this is someone with whom you share a bond. Mark was a principal at a healthcare consulting and brokerage firm—Borislow Insurance—located in my home state of Massachusetts. I hadn't heard of his firm until that day, and I am sure that he didn't know my company either, as The Phia Group was not an industry household name at the time.

A dear colleague of mine has stated in the past that intuition is equal parts experience, empathy, and awareness. Mark demonstrates these qualities like few others. Upon meeting Mark, I noticed right away how he sought to leverage his intuition and passionately face the challenges of our industry head-on. He was not there solely to network or expand his business. Instead, he wanted to facilitate serious, meaningful, positive changes in the realm of health care and health benefits. He unapologetically positioned front and center his concrete, specific goals relating to demanding provider quality and cost transparency. I shared his sentiments and sense of personal responsibility to leave the world better than you'd found it. Truth be told, I might have suffered some whiplash that day, as I was nodding a bit too enthusiastically. It was immediately obvious to me that Mark would be a comrade and a force for good.

So many pundits will tell you that "health care" is too big to wrestle. The issues are so complex, and the web is so tangled, that all we can do is make adjustments in an effort to spread the unavoidable costs across as many people as possible. Mark, like I, has always felt that health care isn't really as complex as you might think. Just like other consumer goods, many of which (like health care) are needed for survival. It simply boils down to supply, demand, and competition. Health care today, however, lacks all elements of consumerism, veiling abuses and excesses behind a wall of fictional complexity and so-called uniqueness. The need for consumerism in health care, however, is today as it was then—an 800-pound gorilla nobody wants to wrestle. Nobody, that is, except for a few unique individuals like Mark Gaunya.

Now is the right time for Mark's way of thinking. Technology is constantly evolving, and the information to which consumers have access is astounding. Other areas of commerce continue to arm the consumer with advanced information and metrics that enable them to buy the best items for the best price. From picking a television to choosing an outfit: cost, quality, customer reviews, and more are at our fingertips. That is, of course, with the exception of health care. Indeed, you and I are better equipped to choose a toothbrush than we are to decide on the pediatrician who will care for our children. Sad. It is simply not sustainable, and Mark was then—as he is now—at the forefront of this important and revolutionary topic.

Since then, our companies—Borislow Insurance and The Phia Group—have worked together to ensure that our mutual clients have all the tools necessary to reduce their overall claim spend while ensuring quality outcomes. I am proud and honored to say that Mark and I have collaborated on so many of the innovative service offerings that are setting the marketplace abuzz. These years of diligent problem-solving have proven to be extremely fruitful for our clients and the millions of people they serve, resulting in countless dollars in yearly health care-related savings achieved through plan design and out-of-the-box thinking.

However, we aren't done yet—and Mark is always eager to collaborate on new opportunities and innovations. That is why, as I became more familiar with the concept of Direct Primary Care (or "DPC"), it was clear to me that Mark would be the perfect advocate for it. I had heard of DPC's growth across places like Texas and Oklahoma, but it wasn't making a splash in some hospital-dominated states—such as my home, the Commonwealth of Massachusetts.

That is when I introduced Mark to another forward-thinking person by the name of Dr. Jeff Gold. Like me, yet another misfit pioneer in the form of Dr. Gold was drawn to Mark's flame. Jeff was the first doctor to establish a DPC clinic in my state—Gold Direct Care in Salem—and he certainly had to clear some hurdles to do so. Subsequent to that introduction, we worked together to identify ways to connect DPC providers with forward-thinking, independent health plans. In doing so, my company became one of the first in the nation to pay its plan members' entire DPC fee. By working with Dr. Gold and other DPC practitioners across the country, we have seen an immediate decrease in overall claim costs, better member outcomes—and most importantly—when our members are sick or need a doctor—they have immediate access to their own doctor who knows their name, their real medical history, and are always available in person, by phone, or via text.

With recent federal legislation clarifying DPC as an HSA-approved expenditure, it is our hope that Mark will continue to disrupt the status quo by introducing forward-thinking concepts—like DPC—to all who will listen. His goal—which we share—is to achieve higher value, accessible primary care while reducing downstream claims. This effort reflects a bigger perspective; specifically, that health care is too often conflated with health insurance. Health insurance is only one method by which we pay for health care. Health care, however, is comprised of more than just the payer. It involves the provider and patient as well. All must align to achieve an optimum health care system. Mark knows that to truly "fix" our health care system for all those who are involved—the patients, the providers of their care, and those who finance it—we must identify ways to empower providers to make the right decisions when it comes to care, empower patients to make informed decisions, and empower benefit plans to pay for care and not for waste.

Like any other social movement in our country, it will take a ground-up approach to truly make a lasting change. We certainly have clear evidence that the top-down approach has not and does not work. Mark has planted so many seeds that have since taken root and expanded into varied flora. Health care—in its entirety—is unique and personal to the patient, their caregiver, family, employer, etc. Mark recognizes this and contemplates ways to achieve individualized results meant to address individual needs. As a clinician first and foremost— and an entrepreneurial "misfit pioneer" (which is a badge we all wear with honor) second—Dr. Gold has learned and continues to learn so much from Mark. In our eyes and many others, he is a colleague, mentor, teacher, role model, visionary, and friend.

As Steve Jobs famously said: "The people who are crazy enough to think they can change the world are the ones who do." Hopefully, the readers of this book will join the village idiots. Whether it was his early interest in DPC as a needle mover or his theories on leadership and fiduciary duties—Mark is a bellwether for us all. Listening to Mark and his guidance has improved my life and the lives of my employees, as well as our families. Mark Gaunya is a true pioneer. His passion and expertise have made The Phia Group, our clients, and the overall industry a better place. An ever-increasing number of employers and brokers are today realizing what we've known all along: The current system cannot continue to proceed as it has. Those, like me, who are fortunate enough to hear what Mark has to say will find themselves ahead of the curve.

—Adam V. Russo, Esq.
CEO, The Phia Group

—Dr. Jeffrey S. Gold
CEO/Owner Gold DirectCare PC

Note to the Reader

IN 2025, THE cost of healthcare for a typical American family of four in an employer-sponsored health plan is $35,119, up from $33,067 in 2024, according to the Milliman Medical Index (MMI).[1] Healthcare costs for the average person increased by 6.7 percent, from $7,378 in 2024 to $7,871 in 2025. Medical and pharmacy costs contributed to 69 percent of the year-over-year cost increase for the average person: $35,119 for a family of four, and $7,871 for an average person. Think about that for a moment. One year of health insurance costs as much as a brand new mid-sized car, and that buying decision happens every year.

Over the past fifteen years, health insurance premiums have increased by no less than 213 percent. At the same time, workers' earnings have only increased by 45 percent against an overall inflation rate of 39 percent.[2] That is unsustainable.

---

[1]   Deana Bell et al. "2025 Milliman Medical Index." *Milliman.* 27 May 2025. https://www.milliman.com/en/insight/2025-milliman-medical-index. Accessed 13 August 2025.

[2]   "Can I Control My Healthcare Costs? 8 Questions You Need to Ask Yourself." *Captivated Health.* https://captivatedhealth.com/wp-content/uploads/2019/05/Captivated-Health-Can-I-Control-My-Healthcare-Costs.pdf.

As if that weren't enough, small and mid-sized businesses pay as much as 18 percent more for the same health benefits provided to larger groups, and out-of-pocket medical costs are the number one reason people file for personal bankruptcy.[3]

An Unsustainable Path

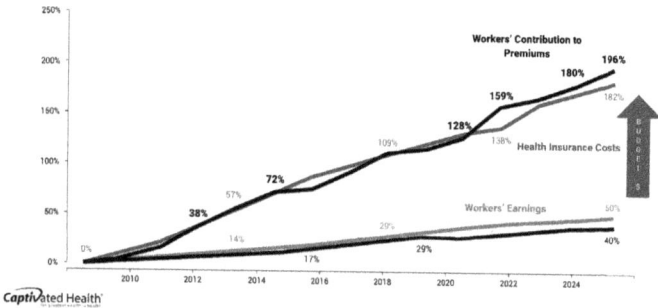

Is healthcare broken? No, it works exactly the way the "rulemakers" designed it. The United States healthcare system was made to serve the institutions that designed it, rather than the consumer—you and me. Every year, premiums rise at an unsustainable rate, feeding the system while employers and consumers struggle to get the healthcare they need at a price they can afford. Instead of adjusting existing algorithms, maybe there is a way to start from scratch through a foundational set of principles and values that put the consumer in the driver's seat instead of the rulemakers.

No, I am not suggesting I can single-handedly overhaul the system, but I can teach you how to hack it by taking control and thoughtfully managing your risk. The Captivated Health Platform[IP] is a **Health Insurance Hacker[IP]**, making

---

3   3 National Conference of State Legislatures

the system work for you. It's elegantly simple, and it requires a shift in how you perceive healthcare and insurance. We'll get into the details later, but for now, here's what you need to know.

We've built our platform around four principles: Members First, Consumerism, Health and Well-being, and Self-Governance. What do they mean? Before anything else, this is about you: the individual healthcare consumer. Every time we look at a potential solution for our clients, we ask, "Would I want that for me or my family?" If the answer is no, we take it off the table and find a better way to **lower costs and create value**.

Second is Consumerism. It is estimated that the healthcare literacy rate in the U.S. is roughly 12 percent, which means almost nine out of ten people have no idea how to speak the language of healthcare.[4] We believe that if we can teach consumers the language and show them how it really works, they can make better, more informed decisions that lead to higher quality and lower costs. This mindset shift gives employers the opportunity to save money on their health insurance by rewarding their employees through incentives for making smarter choices. It's called **strategic alignment**.

Third, we help design and promote a culture of Health and Well-being in the workplace. That means when we work with clients, we assist them in taking a holistic view of helping their people achieve higher levels of physical, financial, workplace, community, and mind and spirit well-being. Through our

---

[4]   Mira Norton, Liz Hamel, and Mollyann Brodie. "Assessing Americans' Familiarity With Health Insurance Terms and Concepts." *Kaiser Family Foundation*, Nov. 11, 2014. https://www.kff.org/affordable-care-act/poll-finding/assessing-americans-familiarity-with-health-insuranc e-terms-and-concepts/. Accessed July 31, 2025.

unique process, we meet employees where they are in those five essential elements and guide them to improve in each area. It's **culture strength training**.

The fourth and most notable principle is self-governance. Our platform is designed to give the employer (plan sponsor) all of the control to achieve their individual and collective goals through a set of bylaws that govern the "risk cell" they participate in. And our risk cells are established with unrelated organizations in a similar industry or affinity group (also known as homogenous risk).

The bylaws are modeled after the United States Senate: each plan sponsor (employer) has one vote, regardless of its size, and any measure (initiative, strategic partner, etc.) that affects the entire risk cell requires a two-thirds majority vote by the participating members to be approved before it is implemented. And like each individual state, every plan sponsor has the freedom to custom-tailor their specific solutions to improve their performance and then share the impact of those solutions with their peers at the Annual Meeting of the Membership.

When the risk cell is formed (at least 3 organizations and 500 total enrolled employees), the plan sponsors elect a Chair and Vice-Chair from the membership (either CFOs or HR professionals) who serve for two years in each role. This structure provides continuity of leadership. Those Chairs govern four committees (governance, finance, membership, and engagement) that are populated with plan sponsor executives. All stakeholders have full visibility into the performance of their own plan as well as the entire risk cell and work collaboratively to better manage the healthcare quality and costs their employees receive so they can all save money. Essentially, our role is to be their health benefits advisor and "intel chip inside," guiding them on their new healthcare journey.

If these foundational principles appeal to you and your organization, then read on.

This book is designed for executive leaders of middle-market employers (50 to 500 employees) who are frustrated with the status quo and the never-ending cycle of the less bad renewal[IP], an annual process where renewal expectations are set by a client's health benefits advisor (broker) who in turn negotiates with the health insurance carrier and obtains bids from the market in an effort to deliver the lowest rate increase possible. On the surface, this sounds like what you would expect in a business transaction. The problem in health insurance lies in the lack of data from the carrier to substantiate the increase and settle on a reasonable price. The result is a less bad renewal.

If you're someone who possesses an entrepreneurial spirit, a strong desire to take control of your health insurance future, and if you are an executive leader (CEO, CFO, HR) who has some insight or responsibility over employees and their healthcare, I ask that you read on with an eye for how Captivated Health® might help you change the game of health insurance for your organization and how you can help make your employees healthier, happier, and more productive and improve your bottom-line at the same time. What if you could 10x your employees' satisfaction by adding benefits and improving the quality of healthcare and support they receive, all while converting your health insurance expense into an asset on your balance sheet?

If you are an executive leader with profit and loss accountability, exploring a new way to finance your health insurance plan could save you money while allowing you the freedom to reinvest the savings back into the benefits of your plan and boost the value of your organization and the goodwill toward your employees at the same time. You've got bottom-line accountability for the financial health of your company, and what you read here could be the Health Insurance Hack[IP] you need to make a real difference to any organization's number one asset: their people.

Even if you don't fall into any of the categories above, maybe you know someone who does, or maybe you just want to learn more about healthcare and insurance. Either way, this book will equip you with everything you need to know about the way our healthcare system was designed, its inherent flaws and other issues surrounding healthcare and insurance, and the best method for hacking the existing system, ending the never-ending cycle of the less bad renewal.

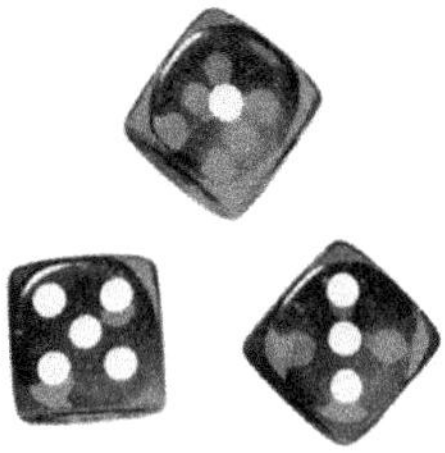

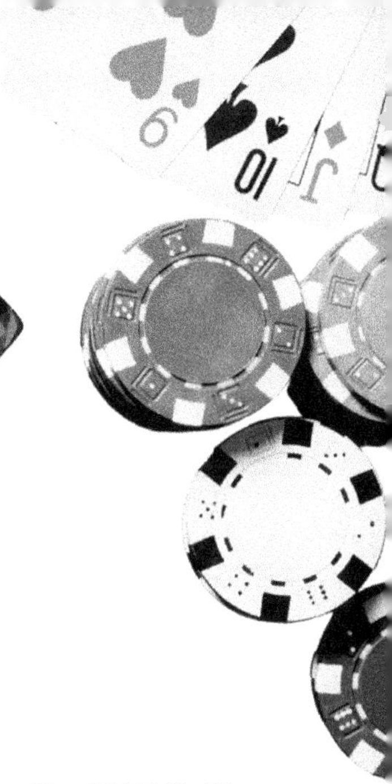

PART 1

The Healthcare Casino[IP]

Risky Business

✳

I N 2011, I trademarked a phrase that pinpoints the root cause of the health insurance cost increase challenge: "Health insurance is expensive because healthcare is expensive."® Some people suggest that there are other factors at play, and while I agree it's not that simple, I always return to the same question: "What is the one thing I would do to solve the problem of rapidly increasing health insurance costs?"

For two decades, my answer has always been the same: "Make price and quality information transparent and easily understood by consumers." It's as simple as that. If you can't see it, how do you measure it? And if you can't measure it, how will you ever improve it? There needs to be a fundamental shift in what we expect and receive when it comes to the quality and cost of healthcare. Think of it this way: name one thing you buy for which you can't access or don't know where to get information on the price or quality before you make a buying decision.

I'll give you a hint: there's nothing. Not your car, not your house, not your groceries, not even something as insignificant as the toy car your toddler begs you to buy. Quality and price, in general, have to be transparent if employers and consumers want to create a sustainable healthcare future. Imagine agreeing to buy a house, but all you know about it is that it has a few bedrooms, maybe two baths, and it might be in a nearby city. Only later do you find out that it costs three times what you wanted to pay, and it's not in very good condition. There's no good reason to enter into a situation where you have zero visibility into what you're getting and how much you're paying for it. It's common sense.

But that's exactly how our healthcare system works— and what's worse is we tolerate it.

For example, let's say you and I both got sick with the same physical ailment and we both visit the same doctor on the same day for treatment. Neither of us knows if the doctor we're seeing is particularly good at treating the type of ailment we have, and there is no data on the quality or price of the service before we have it.

So we have no idea about quality, and we have no idea about price until after we have the service. Does that make any sense?

Now we're both in the doctor's office getting treated, and we present our insurance ID cards to the doctor's office administrative staff. Let's say your health insurance is through "the red card," and mine is through "the blue card," and we have identical benefits. What happens? Roughly three to four weeks later, we both get our Explanation of Benefits (EOB) in the mail and learn that my cost is $100, and yours is $500. Why the difference?

If your first instinct is confusion, closely followed by anger about how unfair that is, you're spot on. The only reason the price for the same service is exponentially different is that my insurance company has a better contract with the doctor's office than yours does, and neither of us knew that before we went to our doctor. It has nothing to do with the quality of care. In fact, unlike every other product or service we buy, **there is no correlation between quality and price in healthcare**. It's about the quality of the contract negotiated, all of which is invisible to us until after we have the service.

The experience feels a lot like a casino where the house always wins. But as it relates to health insurance, this model makes no sense because it doesn't serve the consumer. We are in the middle of a health insurance cost crisis, and it doesn't have to be this way for you. Once you understand the "rules of the game," you can improve your odds in the healthcare casino.

Free Diapers and Wipes for a Better Maternity Experience at a Lower Price

It's been a long time, but I remember the high cost of diapers and wipes for my three children, all under the age of two at one time. Yes, it was a wild ride. And today, that cost pressure is real on a young family. What if I told you a Captivated Health insurance plan could help pay those expenses? One member of the Captivated Health Community, Harpeth Hall—a private, independent all-girls school in Nashville, Tennessee, employing 150 faculty and staff—offered an incentive to its employees, saving $150,000 in one year while improving the experience for expectant mothers. They joined Captivated Health in 2020 and, since then, have emphasized the importance of data-driven decision-making and primary care for its employees.

Harpeth Hall's CFO and COO, Tom Murphy, utilized the transparency of his healthcare claims data to see what could be done to help members and lower costs. With our assistance, he noticed three out of five large claims were related to maternity care and a significant population of female employees and young families on the plan. In Nashville, it can cost up to $100,000 to have a baby, and we're just talking about a normal, problem-free delivery. What can you do to lower costs without sacrificing quality?

When Tom realized they had a huge maternity risk, we helped him negotiate a bundled contract with Vanderbilt University Medical Center, which offers world-class-quality maternity care. Those who opted into the program could receive maternity services at Vanderbilt for the nine-month pregnancy and an additional three months postpartum—a twelve-month maternity concierge service. Expectant mothers received the highest-quality care, and this agreement also saved the school as much as $50,000 per maternity claim. It's a win (mom)-win (baby)-win (school) outcome.

The program is entirely voluntary, the school saves money, and the members have a better experience. Because this program is offered as an option for expectant moms, Tom wanted to add an extra incentive for his employees to sign up, so he decided to use a portion of the savings on these maternity claims to offer free diapers and wipes to enrolled participants for a whole year after the birth. That is a $4,000 value in today's dollars.

If you're a young family, that's thousands of dollars in expenses after tax that you now save if you choose the Vanderbilt Maternity program. Essentially, when organizations use a shared savings model designed by Captivated Health, they empower their employees by saying, "You are making a smarter choice, so I will make sure you have a better experience." The ability to give employees a financial reward for making smarter healthcare decisions makes all the difference. That one strategy immediately helped three families and also created financial savings for the school.

Now, here's the key: Harpeth Hall was able to make a massive impact by switching to the Captivated Health Platform, and instead of giving their employees less each year to lower the less bad renewal, they provided more benefit at a lower cost. That's the kind of impact you can bring to employees if you're willing and able to transform how you think about healthcare and insurance. So let's take a look at what it takes.

Year	Captivated Health Total Costs*	Fully Insured Total Cost†	Approximate Savings Each Renewal
2019	$355,185	$555,611	$200,425
2020	$813,799	$1,111,221	$297,422
2021	$1,202,692	$1,205,675	$2,982
2022	$1,364,603	$1,308,157	($56,446)
2023	$1,170,817	$1,419,350	$248,533
2024	$1,309,414	$1,539,995	$230,581
6-Year Total	$6,216,511	$7,140,009	$923,498

* Fixed Costs, Net Claims, minus Surplus/Rebates, 160 enrollees
† Estimated fully insured renewals based on 8.5% trend, 160 enrollees

The Threat to Your Bottom Line

When you're operating a business, employee benefits will usually be the second-largest expense on the profit and loss (operating) statement, right behind payroll. And that expense grows four to five times faster than any other expense because it has its own inflation rate, also known as the healthcare trend.

Because health insurance premiums grow faster than the ordinary rate of inflation, they erode margin for most businesses. As a non-profit, the old saying is, "No margin, no mission." So in the case of schools, they can't make more seats for kids. Instead, they have to tightly manage their expenses to minimize the need to increase tuition. In fact, according to the National Business Officers Association (School CFOs), every

10 percent increase in health insurance costs is a 1 percent increase in tuition.[5]

If you're a for-profit company, it's just as bad, except you have unhappy shareholders. Rapidly increasing health insurance premiums cut into EBITDA—earnings before interest, taxes, depreciation, and amortization. And again, without a profit margin, employers are forced to raise prices or cut costs in some other way, which is usually reducing the benefits of the health insurance plan through higher premium payroll contributions or higher out-of-pocket costs for their employees. In essence, healthcare and insurance costs are cutting into margins and benefits, and it's happening with very little consideration for the end-user, the consumer.

People tend to forget that **the real customer in healthcare is the individual**. It's you and me, as people. Sure, employers offer health insurance to their employees as a benefit of employment, and they do it to compete for employees. And because of the employer-sponsored health insurance law, health benefits are tax-preferred, which means premium contributions made by employees are deducted before taxes, saving them and their employer money. At the end of the day, employers want employees to be happy, healthy, and, most of all, productive.

It sounds like it's all numbers, profit, and loss. It's really about the benefits to everyone involved. It's for the mothers at Harpeth Hall who now have peace of mind about their maternity experience because they know they're receiving the best care for the best price, and earning a meaningful, creative reward for making a better choice. It's for the employees who get more enhanced mental health care because their employer

---

[5]   Mark S. Gaunya, "A Holistic Approach to Health Benefits." *Net Assets*, 2024. https://www.nboa.org/net-assets/article/a-holistic-approach-to-health-benefits. Accessed July 31, 2025.

noticed a trend in the claims data and did something about it. It's for the diabetic who no longer needs to worry about the affordability of their medication because their participation in their company's health plan helps control those costs and everyone's bottom line.

As I said before, people are the number one asset of any organization. The rapidly increasing rates of traditional healthcare and insurance expenses are a threat to everyone's bottom line. The current system operates inefficiently, diverting financial resources away from organizations and their people. If you're frustrated with the status quo, learn how to squeeze the inefficiency out of healthcare and insurance and then reinvest those savings into things that are helpful and better for people. That is what Captivated Health is all about. It is a **proven platform to help you transform your health plan expense into an asset on your balance sheet**.

2

The Less Bad Renewal

❋

L ET'S BE HONEST. No one really wants to talk about healthcare. People want to wake up in the morning and feel good just like they did the day before. But what happens if they don't and they need to get help from a system that is not built for them? It's a question no one should have to ask for something so incredibly important. But that's the current state of healthcare in America.

Let's say for a moment that I'm your employee benefits insurance broker. I don't really view myself as a broker (advisor), but let's use that term for now, as everyone has a "broker box" in their head. My responsibility is to help you, as the employer, get the most benefits for the lowest possible cost, meeting or exceeding your budget expectations. I might come tell you, "I want you to prepare for a 17 percent increase in your health insurance costs because that is the guidance I received from your health insurance carrier. I'm not saying that's where you'll end up, but that's what I need you to budget."

Your initial reaction is shock and worry, because 17 percent is a massive increase and a hit to your budget. "Is there anything you can do to lower that increase?" you ask.

We respond, "We'll see what we can do." Then we go in and do what most brokers do. We negotiate with the carrier, we underwrite, we analyze what little data we have available, we bid your plan to the market, and we break everything down. In the end, we get the renewal increase reduced to 10 percent.

So I come back to you with the good news: "Remember the renewal guidance we gave you of 17 percent? Well, we reduced it to 10 percent by challenging the underwriting assumptions, taking it out to bid, and using competitive leverage." As your broker, we know it's a better result than you expected and way under the budget you set for the coming year. And we wish we could do better, as that's still four to five times higher than the ordinary rate of inflation.

But hold on. If you take the time to really think about what's happening, you might start comparing other cost increases. If every other expense grows by 2 to 3 percent— the rate of inflation—then even at 10 percent, your health insurance renewal is significantly greater than what it should be under normal business conditions. Because this renewal was framed to you by the health insurance carrier as a massive decrease from what it could have been, the truth is masked. Why? Because **we don't have claim data to substantiate the end result, which means we don't really know if it is the right result; it's just less bad.** We call this the Less Bad Renewal Process. Bad is 17 percent. Less bad is ten. It's still not good enough.

Even if you recognize this unfair process, you don't have the capability to debate the renewal because you don't have any data. In this situation, the carrier controls the information we need to negotiate, including the details of what you're paying for. Still, you're expected to pay the increased renewal premium for the plan or look for ways to further reduce it.

Your next step is to figure out how to pay the increase. The first area you look at is the premium contribution you ask employees to make out of their paychecks for access to the health insurance benefits. Next, you look at increasing deductibles, increasing co-pays, and other areas that add out-of-pocket costs to employees and reduce the financial burden on your organization while shifting it to your people.

The other option, of course, is to switch to a carrier that may offer a lower renewal increase, running from ID card to ID card and away from your renewal with your incumbent carrier. That might work for one year, as you find it to be a great deal to switch. But what happens next year? In many cases, the renewal next year skyrockets to 17 percent again, and you're right back where you started.

The Less Bad Renewal Process is like a hamster wheel. You're stuck running around and around, going nowhere. The faster you run to try to find a solution, the faster the wheel spins. Now imagine a hamster running on his wheel, but he's blindfolded. He doesn't even know he's running in circles. This is exactly what it's like to play the game the way the healthcare system designed it. We run on the track they set up for us, but we're totally blind to the issues we face because we have absolutely no data to give us insight. How could we possibly know if we're being overcharged or not?

Now imagine this Hamster Wheel is in the healthcare casino. We get in the wheel and play their game and hope for a better outcome, knowing in our minds that the house always wins, no matter what we do. So what's the solution? Can we beat the house? Not likely. But there is a better way that will help you to play the game longer and lose less along the way. So let's take a closer look at the designers of this game.

Meet the Rulemaking "Players"

Most people think the health insurance companies are the ones who deserve all the blame for rising health insurance costs—they are the convenient villain. The problem is more complex than that, as they are only one rulemaker in the design. Before we talk about the "players," let's talk about inflation in healthcare.

A big part of the design of the healthcare casino is the creation of its own inflation factor, better known as healthcare trend, which is made up of three components: unit cost, units of service, and provider mix. In layman's terms, the actual cost of healthcare (unit cost), the number of times we use healthcare services (utilization), and the places and people we get that care from (provider mix). Sixty percent of the underlying cause of rapidly rising health insurance is the actual increase in the cost of healthcare services, which are generated from people visiting the hospital, consulting specialists, purchasing prescription drugs, and undergoing tests, imaging procedures, and other medical services.

Through a complex set of algorithms, all of these data elements are combined to calculate the increase in health insurance costs from year to year, and then actuaries and underwriters are responsible for applying those results to the employers who purchase health insurance from them to cover their risk and make a profit. Essentially, insurers add a risk charge (profit) to the premiums they charge clients in exchange for the "easy button" for those clients.

There are three other players at the table who also play in this health insurance game. Together, we call them the Rulemakers. They created the healthcare system and the rules that govern it, and they always win, just like the casino.

The first player is the federal government, which manages Medicare and Medicaid and controls health insurance for about 50 percent of the U.S. population. Medicaid provides for those who cannot otherwise afford health insurance, and Medicare provides for everyone over the age of sixty-five.

There is no way to "hack" the government, as they make the laws and regulations that govern our country. However, it's important to understand their role in this game. The best-kept secret held by the government is the fact that they dictate the level of payment Medicare and Medicaid providers and drugmakers receive when they deliver healthcare to people. And it is well known in the industry that the **government pays about $0.61 to deliver $1.00 of healthcare**. What is the impact? To make up the difference in payment, providers and drugmakers inflate their unit cost and shift those costs to the private market.

This design shifts the payment shortfall to employers and consumers in the form of higher unit cost, which is reflected in premiums and out-of-pocket costs. By now, you might be saying, "The government is in control here, what can I possibly do?" And the answer is to be aware and more knowledgeable about how things work. There are things you can do to reduce the financial pain these programs might cause, but that conversation will be down the road. With that said, the majority of our attention, then, must be focused on the other three players.

Big hospital systems control about 60 percent of the supply of healthcare in every major metropolitan area across our country. In most cases, their brand is very well established, and they own the providers, the doctors, the imaging centers, and almost all other services outside of the pharmacy that we get as healthcare consumers.

If you think it's strange to say hospitals own doctors, don't take my word for it. Look into it. **Hospitals are buying primary care doctor practices because they represent, on average, two million dollars of referrable revenue into the hospital-based system** year in and year out. The doctors refer their patients to the hospital system that owns them, and they direct consumers to facilities and programs owned by the same hospital system in order to keep that revenue in their ecosystem. Those referrals don't always focus on the quality of care for a particular situation or the price of care for that treatment. If your doctor refers you somewhere, your first questions should be, "Is the place you are sending me owned by the hospital?" and "Do you have a financial interest in referring me there?" This is just one way big hospital systems maintain a monopolistic control over their healthcare community. If they control the supply, they also control the price.

The third player is the Prescription Benefit Management companies, or PBMs. These players control access to prescription drugs, which means they also control the prices. I could write an entire book about the fraud, waste, and abuse that goes on in the PBM space, but I won't spend too much time on them in this book because they are one of four players in this game, and we need to tell the whole story. The main issue with pharmaceutical companies is they manufacture many drugs in tier one, English-speaking countries (like Canada, the UK, Ireland, Australia, New Zealand) at a much lower cost and then mark those drugs up for U.S. consumers who end up paying 70 to 80 percent more. It's not ok.

As a quick example, my wife is from Canada. When she buys one of her prescriptions in the U.S., the price is substantially higher than when she buys those same drugs in Canada.

Why? Most drug manufacturers make their drugs overseas at significantly lower costs and ship them over here before they mark them up for us. Essentially, **the United States consumer is subsidizing the rest of the free world for the cost of medications**. It's part of their design, and once again, it puts more pressure on price for the consumer and cost for the employer.

President Trump recently commented on this international market dynamic as he described an interaction with a friend who bought a weight-loss drug in both the United Kingdom and the U.S. According to the President, the drug cost him $88 in the UK, but he paid $1,300 for the same drug in New York City. That's a 1,477 percent increase in price. The location where he received the drug was the only difference, and it is a prime example of how PBMs operate.[6]

The fourth player in this healthcare casino game includes all the health insurance companies, which we refer to as the BUCAs: Blue Cross Blue Shield, United Healthcare, Cigna

---

[6] Beasley, Deena. "Trump calls out weight-loss drugs as target of price-cut push." *Reuters,* May 12, 2025. www.reuters.com/business/healthcare-pharmaceuticals/trump-calls-out-weight-loss-drugs-target-price-cut-push-2025-05-12/. Accessed 2 July 2025.

Healthcare, and Aetna. Health insurance is a risk transfer mechanism designed to protect us from unexpected liability. And in exchange for that protection, we pay insurance premiums. In those premiums, there are risk charges and other administrative costs, including profit margin for the carrier. The majority of the premium (typically 80 percent) is used to pay providers, doctors, hospitals, and PBMs for the delivery of healthcare services and prescription drugs to you and me.

Few debate the importance of insurance. It's a protection every consumer needs. If someone is diagnosed with a rare cancer, the treatment might cost millions of dollars. Without insurance, that cancer treatment cost would be enough to cause bankruptcy. Insurance itself is necessary and beneficial. **The problem is the health insurance companies do not have any incentive to reduce the cost of care because in their casino, more healthcare services equal more profit.** To exacerbate the problem, insurance companies do not provide transparency of price or quality, which exacerbates that problem for employers and their people. They have no idea what they're paying for. And that is unacceptable.

As noted earlier, health insurance is expensive because healthcare is expensive. Between the government, the hospital systems, and the PBMs, the costs pile up, and the insurance companies charge increasingly higher premiums to cover those cost increases.

Now that you understand the Four Rulemakers, we need to ask how they make the system work the way it does. How do prices spiral upward without any reprieve? Everything the Four Rulemarkers do is opaque, as if behind a curtain. And that lack of transparency creates a dynamic most people are not aware of. Let's say you and I have the same healthcare benefits plan design being offered through different employers and insurance companies, and we are being treated for the same condition by the same provider. Did you know that the price for those services could be vastly different? You would probably say, "No, I had no idea. All the details are not available to me until after I get the care I need."

Health insurance carriers build provider networks (doctors, hospitals, labs, etc.) for us to access all necessary healthcare services. Each one of those carriers negotiates a contract (usually three years) for a full range of services, and then a billing code, called a CPT code, is assigned to that service inside the algorithm. When someone goes to the doctor, a CPT code is applied, and that code corresponds with a contractually negotiated discount, so the health insurance carrier is not paying the gross charge. There are thousands of codes used to bill and collect for services, and that code is sent from the doctor's office to the insurance company to inform them about what was done to you and me. In turn, that triggers a payment to the provider based on the contract that was negotiated by that insurance company. There is nothing wrong with the mechanics in this process. It works exactly as it was designed. It's the lack of transparency of price and quality **before** the healthcare service is delivered that we deserve to know.

We all hope when we are not well that we're receiving good care, but quality is often undisclosed to us. Most people rely on their doctor for guidance and support, and that's a good thing most of the time, when the doctor is acting in our best interests. Everyone should ask their doctor one question: "Do you have a financial interest in the facility or drug that you are prescribing for me?" And the follow-up questions include, "Does the drug you are prescribing me or the location you're sending me to offer the highest quality care for my specific health condition? How many people like me out of a hundred has this treatment helped, and how many has it harmed?"

These questions inform and protect us from the powerful dynamic of marketing and branding in healthcare. Most people tend to go to hospitals that are large and well-known, completely unaware of the fact that those brand name places may not offer the best care for a given specific condition. We associate a powerful brand with high quality, and that is not always an accurate assumption. In fact, it's false in most cases.

In the final analysis, a **lack of transparency only serves the system and not the people**. That is why the Consolidated Appropriations Act of 2020, which makes transparency of price and quality the law of the land, is such a game changer for employers and their people. The rules of the healthcare casino help the Four Rulemakers make a profit, but they don't help us. It's high time to hack the system. Read on to learn how.

PART 2

✴

The Hack

3

The Health Insurance Hacker

✳

L ET'S TAKE A peek at the health insurance situation for most middle-market companies. First, meet Mary, the CFO. She is watching health insurance costs rise endlessly and feels like she's losing control of the situation. Employee benefits are her second biggest expense behind payroll. They grow four times faster than any other expense, and the system gives her very little information and zero leverage to find a better answer. She does everything she can to manage the cost, even if it means reducing the benefits for her employees or taking more money out of their paychecks in the form of higher premium contributions. All she wants is sustainability, predictability, transparency, and the ability to plan long-term rather than just react each year to the less bad renewal.

Then there's Amy, the HR professional. She is the person the employees lean on to help with their benefits, and she is exhausted, dealing with mental health challenges, serious illnesses, and the high cost of medication for her people at the company, and she is struggling to engage employees. Every change she makes in an attempt to make things better is disruptive and sometimes painful. Those changes cause friction and result in unhappy people. She wants to provide a better employee experience and benefits that grow in value, but she doesn't have the tools to support her team, not to mention the budget.

Finally, let's talk about Joe, the employee. His situation is also challenging as he gets less and pays more every year. He's confused and frustrated with his health insurance benefits. He doesn't know how to use them, he doesn't trust the system, and he ends up spending more than he should and getting less in the way of quality. Despite Mary and Amy's efforts, Joe does not feel like anyone is on his side.

The current model is not working for most people at this company. What can Mary and Amy do? The traditional solutions are to switch carriers to reduce the impact of the annual renewal, change the plan design by adding higher deductibles and co-pays, shifting more cost to Joe, or increase their employee per-paycheck premium contributions. None of these tactics will help anyone in the long run. Most middle market employers are in a similar situation. They are unaware of all their options, so they default to running in the healthcare casino hamster wheel to receive the less bad renewal. If Mary knew there was a hack for escaping this process, it would change her perspective on everything. It would give her control of her healthcare future.

Fully Insured Health Insurance Financing Is a Trap

Let's separate the health insurance plan(s) you offer your employees (benefit plan design) and focus on how you finance (pay for) your health insurance plan.

Healthcare Financing
High Level Contrast

	THE INSURANCE COMPANY	YOUR INSURANCE COMPANY (Partially Self-funded)
RISK	Transfer	Assume, Share, Transfer
PREMIUM	Pay *(includes tax and insurance company profits)*	Pay claims, administrative costs and premium *(keep any excess)*
DATA	Little or none	Full access
TREND	Higher	Lower
CONTROL	None	Full

Capti√ated Health

As a middle-market employer, you have four options for financing your health insurance benefits. First, you can select the traditional model by being fully insured through a health insurance company. In this financing model, you are transferring all of your risk, even the good risk, to the insurance company in exchange for a predictable premium every month for twelve months of the year. Those premiums include tax on 100 percent of that premium and a healthcare trend that is much higher than the rate of overall inflation. At the end of those twelve months, you will receive a less bad renewal, very little data on why the premiums and rates are going up, and no control over your choices to solve the root problem next year.

If you have an open checkbook to spend on health insurance, maybe being fully insured doesn't sound too bad. It's the easy button. That's great. However, if you're like most people and have reasonable limits on your health insurance budget, there are other options.

The second way you can finance your health insurance plan is through a level-funded financing strategy. This financing method requires an employer to transition into partial self-insurance. The main difference here is that you are using stop-loss insurance to protect yourself from large healthcare expenses like cancer treatment or the premature delivery of twins. Stop-loss coverage is not health insurance. It is property and casualty insurance. It insures the employer (plan sponsor) from excess loss, so if any one person covered by your health insurance plan has a significant health risk issue, you are reimbursed for the extra costs above your company's limit of liability (known as specific stop loss per covered person on the plan). Or, if a lot of people get sick, there is a limit of liability on your entire organization (known as aggregate stop loss to provide a limit of liability for the entire company). When an employer is self-insured, they are largely governed by ERISA (The Employee Retirement Income Security Act of 1974) rather than the Affordable Care Act.

Captive self-insurance, the third option and the focus of this book, is very similar to a traditional stop-loss arrangement for self-insured financing. If you are a large company with 10,000 employees, you don't buy stop-loss insurance. The law of large numbers makes costs very predictable for underwriters, and you don't need a stop-loss carrier to reimburse you for large claims because of that predictability. If you are an employer with 50 to 500 employees, however, the law of large numbers doesn't work quite as well, introducing more volatility of high-cost claims and making it necessary to hedge your bets with stop-loss coverage. And the hedge to those less predictable high-cost claims is called the captive layer, which is a layer of risk sharing across the captive cell on the group purchasing platform. Essentially, the captive layer is stop-loss coverage that is pooled. This shared layer of risk is what makes the captive structure creative, as it allows unrelated employers to individually self-insure and then share risk with one another.

There are **three risk transfer mechanisms built into the self-insured captive structure,** which is what makes it unique and attractive to plan sponsors, as it gives them a defined limit of financial responsibility. The first risk transfer mechanism is designed for one single large claim. Let's say one of the plan participants experiences the premature delivery of twins, which costs $500,000. A self-insured captive structure requires the plan sponsor to pay a defined portion ($50,000), the captive layer to pay a portion ($300,000), and the stop-loss carrier to pay the remaining balance ($150,000). The second risk transfer mechanism is designed to put a limit on the plan sponsor's entire liability, and once it reaches a certain threshold (typically 120 or 125 percent of total expected claims), that risk is transferred to the stop-loss insurer. And the final risk transfer mechanism is designed to put a limit of liability on all of the participants in a captive, protecting every plan sponsor's downside risk.

Captive Self-Funding

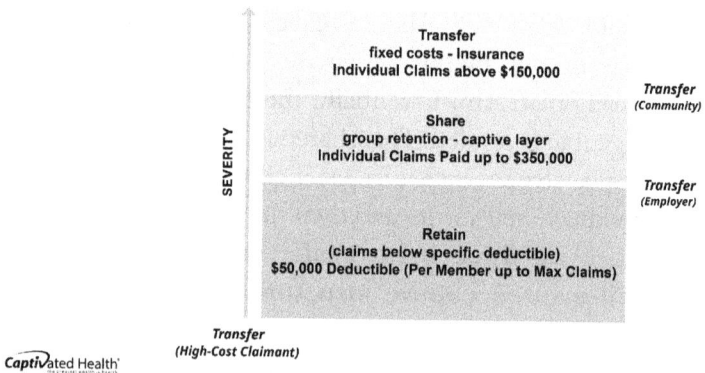

A quick note about the members of a self-insured captive: From a risk management perspective, it is safer to share risk with a homogeneous (same industry, association, or franchise) group of employers. Reports show that when grouped with like-minded organizations, plan sponsors gain more purchasing power and yield more predictable outcomes while diversifying risk exposure.[7] The more similar the captive members are, the more predictable and manageable the costs will be because there is commonality in the demographics among similar groups of employers, not to mention language that is unique to that industry. For example, our Captivated Health Education Cell includes thirty private independent schools in seven states that are all individually self-insured and refer to their employees as faculty and staff. They aren't related to one another, and they don't share any business interests, but they do refer to employees with the same language and collectively

---

7 "Stop Loss: State of the Market Report." *Stealth Partner Group.* Mat 2025.

share health insurance risk with one another in order to be treated like a life group of 10,000 instead of 100.

When you create scale, you drive down fixed costs, and you can anticipate major claim costs more accurately because the members are all schools with a similar demographic profile. At the end of the day, captive self-insurance creates a **"high-cost claim volatility shock absorber"** to protect each of the plan sponsors from bearing the full financial exposure of expensive healthcare claims.

The last insurance financing option takes independence in group health insurance one step further with standalone self-insurance. If a company is large enough (1,000 or more) for the law of large numbers to apply, then it may not want to share that risk with other organizations, as it manages its health insurance benefits alone. The same concepts of managing risk and implementing solutions to mitigate that risk exist for standalone plan sponsors; they are just not sharing risk with other organizations to create the scale they already enjoy.

Traditional Insurance Models vs. Captive Models

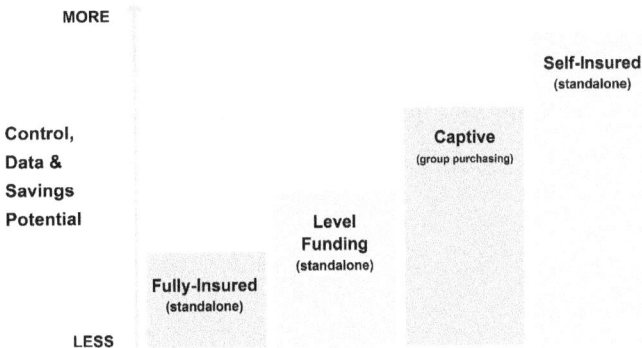

*Captiv*ated Health

We've already seen how being fully insured operates like a hamster wheel in the healthcare casino. If you remain in the wheel, your health insurance carrier will continue to raise premiums year after year, and you will continue to receive very little explanation for the reason for those increases. They will maintain their own profit margin, and they will also charge you for state premium tax on your entire premium, per law. As a result, your costs are higher, and you have no control or visibility into what's driving those cost increases and negatively impacting your profit and loss statement.

When an employer decides to take control of their health insurance plan, they exit the hamster wheel by leaving the fully insured market. From there, if they prefer to go it alone, they transition to level funding or standalone self-insurance financing (assuming they are big enough). If, however, they want to leverage scale and collaborate on a group purchasing platform, a captive financing structure is the ideal solution.

The Captive Difference

There are three things you can do with health insurance risk: retain it, share it, or transfer it. In a self-insured captive model, you get to do all three with other employers who are like you, who think like you do, and who want to do things collectively, as a team.

Changing the Rules
Improve your odds by understanding the game

	Fully-Insured (Traditional Insurance)	Captive Models (Partially Self-Funded Captive)
RISK	*100% transferred to carrier*	Shared risk, employer retains control
PREMIUM	*Fixed annual payment (carrier profits either way)*	Fund claims, admin, and keep your savings
DATA	*Minimal access*	Full access and real-time insights
TREND	*High and unpredictable*	Lower and manageable
CONTROL	*None*	Full control over design, funding, and strategy

Capti*v*ated Health

Together, you get to hack the healthcare system. Instead of being a victim of the less bad renewal and all the frustrations and financial challenges involved, you get to take your health insurance plan expense and turn it into an asset. And that asset now provides you with four key benefits:

- **Control**: As you move **from system-decision to self-decision**, you have the authority to make the best healthcare choices for your company and employees.

- **Transparency**: What you don't know *can* free you, and with the data in your hands, you can make informed, quality-focused, cost-conscious decisions.

- **Confidence**: When you **speak the language**, you can **influence the outcome**. Your increased control and access to data allow you and your employees to build your healthcare literacy so you can create the best outcomes.

- **Cash**: As the hack saves you money, you can reinvest your dividends (surplus) to create greater value for you, your company, and your employees.

Let's return to Mary, Amy, and Joe. If their company joins a self-insured captive, we can immediately see how these benefits solve their health insurance cost and quality concerns. Mary now has budget sustainability and predictability. She knows exactly what she is financing, and she can tailor her benefits for ultimate effectiveness and efficiency. Amy can reinvest the saved money by providing employees with better benefits and lower per paycheck contributions, supporting retention, recruitment, mental health, and engagement. Joe has improved, personalized benefits, smart tools, and a reason to care about being a smarter healthcare consumer.

Let's take a closer look at each step of the Health Insurance Hacker to see how your story could be just like Mary, Amy and Joe's.

4

Take Control

Move from System-Decision to Self-Decision

❋

O NE OF MY clients, John, is a CFO who switched to Captivated Health six years ago. He called me one day and said, "Mark, do you know that my health insurance costs are the same now as they were six years ago?"

I replied, "Yes, I'm aware of that," still not exactly sure where this conversation was heading.

"That's never happened in my professional life! I have a hundred employees and spend about a million dollars each year on our health insurance, and right now, I have a million and a half dollars in my bank account."

" . . . And?" I asked.

"This will pay my health insurance costs for the entire year." His voice was increasingly strained as he reflected back to all the years of the less bad renewal.

"Okay . . . why are you getting upset about it?"

"I'm upset because I've been getting ripped off for years! I'm thinking about all the years we didn't do it this way, and the reality that I left *millions* on the table!"

He was really getting elevated now, so I reassured him that he wasn't throwing away money anymore and reminded him he was in a good spot now. Thinking back on that call later, I just smiled. Who gets calls like that? This is just one example of how shocking the difference can be when you **no longer allow the system to make decisions for you and you take control**.

Sure, when you are fully insured, you get to transfer 100 percent of your risk in exchange for budget predictability, and the result is you may end up like John, letting millions be added to the insurance company's bottom line instead of your own.

Moving from system-decision to self-decision is a powerful shift, and it is not a change to be made lightly. It's important to understand all the factors involved when you decide to take control into your own hands. With opportunity comes responsibility.

Switching Your Financing Mechanism

Before you can make any decisions, you must understand the differences between the four methods of financing your health insurance plan. These are the four options we looked at in the last chapter. If you're leaving the fully insured hamster wheel, your other three options are all flavors of self-insurance. No matter which of the three you choose, you will, in large part, exit being governed by the Affordable Care Act and instead transition to be governed by ERISA, which is what large organizations with thousands of employees are governed by. You can't get off the hamster wheel unless you take this first, all-important step.

The question is "Do you want to go it alone or do you want to leverage the power of group purchasing and the law of large numbers?" If you're looking to go it alone, you have two options: level-funding or standalone self-insurance, assuming your company is big enough. If you'd prefer to collaborate with other like-minded employers and leverage the scale and insight of many, then a group captive is for you. There are some best practices you can use to choose one over the other. The Captivated Health Report Card provides a list of elements every plan sponsor should evaluate before entering into a captive model, and to no one's surprise, the Captivated Health Platform satisfies all the requirements and is considered by many to be best-in-class.

The Captive Report Card

For a complete, downloadable Report Card, visit CaptivatedHealth.com/Book or scan the following QR code.

At Borislow Insurance, we have over a hundred independent private schools in our book of business. Thirty of them are in Captivated Health for Education, while the others are doing something different. There's no right or wrong answer; there is only a right fit and a wrong fit.

If you're still unsure which path is the right fit for you, try answering these questions:

- Does your C-suite view controlling health insurance costs as a major organizational priority?
- Is providing employee benefits integral to the success of your organization?
- Are you willing to assume some calculated risk? Do you see self-funding as an opportunity to take control and reduce health insurance costs?
- Is your organization financially sound?
- Do you have fifty enrolled employees on your health insurance plan?
- Over the past two to three years, have your health insurance renewal increases been less than 10 percent?
- Do you provide your employees with ongoing benefit education and clear communication before and after open enrollment?

- Do you view your health insurance costs as a direct result of the decisions your employees make about the healthcare they access?

Take some time to consider your answers and the implications of each question for you, your employees, and your organization. If you answered "yes" to most of these questions, you're in a great place to consider captive self-insurance.

Joining a group captive is the best way to proceed if your organization is too small to benefit from the risk protection of the law of large numbers on its own, and you want more control and data than a level-funded plan can offer.

Ongoing Involvement

Now you've taken the first step towards hacking the system. You've assumed control by switching your health insurance financing structure to self-insurance. The responsibility, however, doesn't end there.

The Captivated Health Platform truly shines when an employer and their employees want to take control of their health insurance future and **create a long-term, data-driven, results-oriented culture.** We've found that the best way to create and maintain such a system is to establish a self-governing body for members of each risk cell. As a member of a captive, you have a direct say in every change that directly affects you. Whether evaluating prospective members, changing the plan design, adding consumerism tools, or any other major adjustment, you get to weigh in on the decision based on what would best help your organization. At the same time, as a collection of employers, there will be decisions to make that affect every member of the captive cell, and when those important choices are presented, there is a governance structure (two-thirds majority vote) that is required to pass any measure affecting the entire cell.

Essentially, you become the owner of your own dedicated health insurance company in which the member organizations make the decisions that govern the community. Every member organization has an equal vote, regardless of size. To ensure this balance of representation, we form an Executive Committee that includes a Chair and Vice Chair (who serve two consecutive two-year terms) as well as four committees (Governance, Finance, Membership, and Engagement) populated by high-level staff from member organizations to help govern and keep everyone informed during the year.

To further the feeling of community, we also hold an Annual Meeting of the Membership for all participating organizations, offering the opportunity to collaborate, share best practices, learn what new techniques and technologies are happening in the marketplace, and vote on any changes they want made in their captive program, importantly leaving autonomy and flexibility to choose what's best at the member level.

In a captive, your control extends far past that initial decision to use captive self-insurance. On the Captivated Health Platform, you get to take an active role in the governance of health insurance decisions as long as you are partnered with other like-minded organizations that seek to promote the best structure and benefits for those who rely on them.

Case Study: Lisa A. Brothers, Past President and CEO of Nitsch Engineering, in her own words, on taking less out of her people's paychecks

Nitsch Engineering was founded in 1989 to deliver collaborative, cost-effective solutions in civil, transportation, and structural engineering, as well as green infrastructure, land surveying, and GIS. I served as the President and CEO of Nitsch from 2011 until 2024, during which time we switched to using a captive for health insurance.

When Nitsch was fully insured, we would go to market every year to get quotes from three carriers. We always had an increase. We tried everything to relieve the pressure of the extra cost: we made changes to the plan, upped the contributions, we even limited the plan to make it more affordable. Costs got so bad that when we went to market in 2016, one of our carriers declined to give us a quote, so we were down to only two carriers.

Then Jennifer Borislow of Borislow Insurance gave me a call and told me about this Captivated Health platform. They were trying to start an engineering risk cell and wanted us to help create it. It was a whirlwind to try to figure out what everything meant and what our insurance would look like once we were part of the captive, but Borislow's team helped educate us and clarify everything we needed to know.

We took control, and we were one of the founders of the engineering risk cell in 2017, and I am happy to share the numbers so you can see what our health insurance looked like and what we saved as a result of making the switch. Unfortunately, we did have a high cost claim the same year we joined the captive, which hurt our health insurance plan financial performance and took us to the max on our costs. We actually lost money in the first year. Still, as we were looking at the numbers and the impact of that large claim, we realized that if we had been fully insured in 2017 and gone over with that large claim, we would have seen not just the typical 8.5 percent trend increase in our costs, we would most certainly have had a double-digit increase.

Year	Captivated Health Total Costs*	Fully Insured Total Cost†	Approximate Savings Each Renewal
2017	$943,792	$894,754	($49,038)
2018	$963,089	$970,808	$7,720
2019	$832,571	$1,053,327	$220,756
2020	$822,785	$1,142,860	$320,074
2021	$834,402	$1,240,003	$405,601
2022	$1,031,666	$1,345,403	$313,737
2023	$1,151,646	$1,459,762	$308,117
7-Year Total	$6,579,951	$8,106,918	$1,526,967

* Fixed Costs, Net Claims, minus Surplus/Rebates
† Estimated fully insured renewals based on 8.5% trend

Because every year stands on its own in captive self-insurance, we actually got money back the next year in the form of a surplus. As the years went on, we kept saving more and more money compared to what we would have spent being fully insured. That money we saved went back into the company's bank account rather than straight to a health insurance company bottom line.

What I love most about Captivated Health is we stayed with the same carrier network of doctors and hospitals when we enrolled in the platform, and there were no changes in provider access for our team. We kept the same robust benefit plan we always had, and because we started saving money, we have been able to **keep our employee premium contribution increases flat over the past five years**. In fact, we've even started to reduce our employee premium contributions over the last two years. I don't know how many engineering firms out there can say that they have actually been able to reduce the cost of health insurance that their employees are contributing to the plan without sacrificing any plan quality or benefits. We have had enough savings to be able to enhance our plan benefits, and that is the magic behind this health insurance solution.

Everyone has good years and bad years, but because we are in a self-insured captive, we can all share the risk amongst everyone in the captive, and there are plenty of liability protections built in that add extra security without sacrificing independence. Those protections limit our liability for every individual high-cost claim and put a cap on our company's liability if we have a bad year. Because of the control the Captivated Health Platform gave us, we could craft our plan exactly the way we wanted. I can't even imagine where we'd be right now, what kind of poor coverage we would have, and what we'd be paying for it if we had stayed fully insured.

5

Gain Transparency

What You Don't Know Can Free You

✳

HE FIRST THING that will happen after you take
control of your health insurance plan is you will
have access to your claims data (in the aggregate, not
person by person), which will help you better understand what
you are paying for. When you are fully insured, this data is
not shared with you because the health insurance company is
taking all of the risk in exchange for taking all of the control.

Why? Withholding data benefits the insurance company and undermines your ability to negotiate a fair renewal.
There's an old adage: if you can't see it, you can't measure it or
improve it. And this dynamic favors the insurance company as
long as you are still running around on the hamster wheel with
a blindfold on.

Embracing transparency changes everything. As soon
as you transition your financing to become self-insured, you
can rip the blindfold off to see exactly what you're paying
for and why. Every dollar is visible to you. And if you can
see it, you can measure it, and if you can measure it, you can
improve it.

Transparency is eye-opening. Ultimately, it gives you more than just knowledge. Out in the market, I often hear, "Transparency doesn't work." And my response is transparency isn't a thing; **it's a principle that things are created from**. Once you leave the world of unawareness and enter the world of awareness, you can't return to being unaware. Transparency of your data gives you the opportunity to act responsibly with your healthcare dollars, which is what the plan participants expect. In fact, when you transition into self-insurance, you get two new titles: plan sponsor and Fiduciary. When you transition into self-insurance, you become the plan sponsor, so officially, you have fiduciary responsibility for your insured employees and their families, who are called plan participants. Adding that title scares a lot of people because it sounds like there's liability involved, and there is, but it can be tightly managed. And with the right guidance, you can readily mitigate that liability by scientifically managing your risk.

As the plan sponsor, you are now managing all the assets of the health insurance plan, which includes the premium contributions your people make each pay period to participate in the plan, as well as the ones the company makes to buy health insurance for its people. Essentially, you are responsible for managing that healthcare capital. And it is your responsibility to assess how the plan is performing and determine how it can continue to serve the plan participants.

Let's say you are an employee at my organization who just transitioned to self-insurance. You are now a plan participant in a self-funded plan, which is largely governed by ERISA. What would your expectations be, knowing that your employer is now directly managing your health insurance? You probably expect that I, as the plan sponsor, keep your health information confidential and secure and manage your money with your best interests in mind. After all, you're putting money in, so you should benefit. You'd have a serious problem if I started using excess money from the plan to go on wild vacations or give myself lavish bonuses or pay other bills that don't directly impact you.

A responsible plan sponsor will reinvest savings back into the plan to benefit the members. Maybe it's for a better pharmacy program, mental health program, orthopedic surgery program, maternity program, or whatever best serves the needs of the employees. Here's the key, though. You would never be able to reasonably expect that of your employer unless your company is self-insured. If your employer is fully-insured, the health insurance company is the plan sponsor, and they have all the control and unlimited access to health plan data. Most fully insured employers wouldn't have the visibility into their health insurance plan data to be able to identify needs and proactively make changes to improve the value because they rely on the health insurance carrier to make those decisions.

A significant source of frustration arises from this: the employee wants a supportive health insurance plan, and the employer lacks the data to determine where extra support is needed or even what costs and benefits are being utilized effectively. If the employer opts to take on calculated risk, mitigate that risk with stop-loss insurance, and become self-insured, then they have the data and control necessary to **optimize the health insurance plan** for the benefit of all involved.

The Data Engine

When you enter into a captive self-insured arrangement, it's essential to understand how you get access to the data for your plan. As a plan participant, HIPAA (Health Insurance Portability and Accountability Act) protects the privacy and confidentiality of your personal health information, which means the plan sponsor doesn't get the specific health claims data of individuals. **Information is never personally identifying**. Instead, a sophisticated data analytics engine is deployed to provide the plan sponsor with the necessary information to effectively manage the plan while protecting the privacy of plan participants.

The Captivated Health Platform uses a state-of-the-art data analytics and reporting system, which manages all your information if you are part of the plan. Anytime you present your ID card, whether you are buying a drug, going to the hospital, having a surgery, or treating the flu, the claim data is fed into this system. The actual claim is adjudicated by a Third-Party Administrator (TPA), who applies the network discounts that have been negotiated, depending on which BUCA network your employer selected for you.

From there, the data is shared with plan sponsors through our analytics engine as non-person-specific data. The plan sponsor gets gross claim amounts, negotiated discounts, net claims, and all the diagnoses. They also receive a risk score for each member covered by the plan. One person might have a risk score of less than one, which would make them a favorable risk. Someone else might have a risk score of 1.5, which would indicate a less-than-favorable risk. Again, there is no personally identifying indication of what makes a specific person a favorable or unfavorable risk; that information is protected within the system. The data helps the plan sponsor understand their risk profile and then build strategies to mitigate that risk.

In many cases, we find that the dependents of company employees—spouses and children—have less attractive risk scores than the employees themselves. But no one could know that unless they had the data. The best of intentions might have you adding benefits and programs that would never even appeal to your plan participants, much less solve any real issues.

Plus, even if you did know about the issue, you wouldn't be able to do anything about it under a fully insured plan, as the insurance company has all the control.

With the data, you can be scientific about how you help your people. If you're noticing a rising trend of mental health issues among the dependents of your employees, you can do something about it. You can remove the blindfold, step off the hamster wheel, and add value to a situation that people care deeply about. Transparency can change lives. You have to be willing to take on some calculated risk and assume responsibility.

Of course, there are practical steps you must take to ensure privacy and confidentiality. Everything must be protected by HIPAA, and you also need to make sure that whatever platform you utilize for data analysis is SOC 2-compliant, which simply ensures the platform has the appropriate cybersecurity measures to guarantee privacy and confidentiality. There is a lot of sensitive data involved in healthcare: social security number, date of birth, address, medical history, and any diagnoses. It's crucial to ensure any entities or organizations you work with place a premium on making sure all data is protected.

Case Study: Dirk DeRoo, Director of Compensation and Benefits at Phillips Exeter Academy, in his own words, on re-investing the dividends

Phillips Exeter Academy is a private secondary boarding school in Exeter, NH. We joined Captivated Health in 2017 with 700 employees, 500 of whom were benefits-eligible. The fully-insured plan we had before would be folding within two years. We had to make a change. We explored three options before switching our health insurance financing to a self-insured captive model.

Prior to Captivated Health, we had no access to our claims data. We felt as though our claims experience wasn't the best, but there was no way to know. Once we made the switch, the data analytics engine took us on a deep dive into our claims. We learned the trends, the high diagnostic categories, the incident rates, and facility patterns, all while protecting the confidentiality and security of our enrollees. **From that data, we found a higher-than-average incidence of mental health claims.** These claims were evident in our adults and, sadly, in the **teenage dependents** population as well. Now that we knew, we had an obligation to do something about it if we were going to be a responsible employer (plan sponsor).

Our solution was to tap into our own in-house mental health counselors. We have six clinicians, master's, and PhD-level in-house mental health counselors. And because they were already serving our teenage population at the school, what would be better than to have those same resources help our enrolled employees? We ran thirty-minute Zoom webinars over four straight weeks. These were so well-received that we did another round of education in the fall and spring.

We also introduced Calm, the nation's number one mental health app, at no cost to our employees. We're able to fund Calm by using surplus dollars from the captive layer as well as pharmacy rebates. Our employees are thrilled with Calm. Our enrollment rate is 52 percent, and our engagement rate is 75 percent.

In our claims data, we also noticed a **higher-than-average incidence of MSK** (musculoskeletal, hips, knees, backs), mental health, and metabolic claims. Right as we were discovering this, Captivated Health introduced a digital point solution designed for, of all things, those very three conditions. Just as we did with Calm, we were able to fund DARIO at no cost to our employees by taking the surplus dollars from the captive layer and pharmacy rebates from prescription drugs our people were taking, and funneling those resources into that program. Now we have over a hundred people enrolled in it, receiving online solutions and health coaching in nutrition and exercise. **They are getting the help they need, and we are lowering costs for the plan.**

When we consider wellness from a holistic viewpoint, we obviously look at the physical, emotional, and social aspects, but there's also financial wellness. Over the last seven to ten years, the whole arena of financial wellness has become widely popular. So at no cost to our employees and fully funded through the captive surplus dollars, we offer North Star. Now, employees have unlimited access to Certified Financial Planners—the highest designation in the field of financial advising. Employees can call, Zoom, email, or chat as many times as they want with their advisor on topics like investments, taxes, budgeting, benefit plans, and mortgages, all at no cost to them. If you were to get a full financial plan on the open market, it could cost anywhere between $3,000 and $10,000, depending on the complexity of that portfolio. And again, we **provide that value to our employees at no cost to them**.

To support the plan participants through their healthcare journey, we also introduced Rightway®, a concierge service enabling our employees to find information about their healthcare options. They can pick up the phone or go to the Rightway app and engage with a clinician to learn about their choices and actions to take as a well-advised consumer. A huge part of that is enabling transparency. What is the typical price of an MRI? What information on quality measures is available? Rightway also troubleshoots claims. They can provide a physician locator service. Adding this service increased satisfaction and improved our employee experience significantly.

I see healthcare as more of a transactional experience. Look, we don't think about health insurance when we're working. We just don't. Employee health plans lurk in the background. Oh, but when I trip over a vacuum cord and break my arm or I go in for meniscus knee surgery, now I'm involved in a transaction and suddenly have to think about all the factors that come with healthcare. What's my out-of-pocket going to run me? Is that what they call "deductible?" What's my plan going to pay? And who do I call for answers? HR? Rightway? These numbers on the back of my ID card? It's all very confusing. So, knowing there are levers to pull, such as Rightway for transparency and clinical guidance or DARIO for targeted health conditions, we hope to create a positive user experience and simplify the process and give our employees the tools to become better consumers.

Year	Captivated Health Total Costs*	Fully Insured Total Cost†	Approximate Savings Each Renewal
2017	$8,344,050	$9,098,932	$754,882
2018	$9,600,934	$9,112,931	($488,003)
2019	$8,078,704	$9,887,530	$1,808,826
2020	$9,616,271	$10,727,970	$1,111,699
2021	$9,259,167	$11,639,847	$2,380,680
2022	$10,081,534	$12,629,234	$2,547,701
2023	$11,557,570	$13,702,719	$2,145,149
2024	$11,760,959	$14,867,450	$3,106,491
8-Year Total	$78,299,189	$91,666,615	$13,367,426

* Fixed Costs, Net Claims, minus Surplus/Rebates
† Estimated fully insured renewals based on 8.5% trend, 750 employees

6

Leverage Confidence

Speak the Language to Influence the Outcome

✴

A CCORDING TO THE Kaiser Family Foundation, the **healthcare literacy rate in the United States is around 12 percent.** That means nine in ten adults struggle to use the healthcare system effectively and knowledgeably.[8] Most can't even speak the language of healthcare, let alone become informed healthcare consumers!

How well do your employees know what is going on when they go to the doctor and hand over their insurance ID card? Do they know what the quality and price of their options are? Is there any incentive to research treatments, facilities, and doctors in order to find the best care? Or are they at the mercy of the system, limited by the lack of transparency and available knowledge?

---

[8]   Mira Norton, Liz Hamel, and Mollyann Brodie. "Assessing Americans' Familiarity With Health Insurance Terms and Concepts." *Kaiser Family Foundation*, Nov. 11, 2014. https://www.kff.org/affordable-care-act/ poll-finding/assessing-americans-familiarity-with-health-insuranc e-terms-and-concepts/. Accessed July 31, 2025.

You can make a big impact on your employees' health-care literacy simply by utilizing the **best practices outlined in** *Bend the Healthcare Trend*, a book I co-authored with Jennifer Borislow on how to create a culture of consumerism, health, and well-being in the workplace and engage and reward your employees (plan participants) when they make smarter decisions. This book is a **practical guide for employers** that explains each step and then illustrates the impact of those steps through actual client case studies in each chapter.

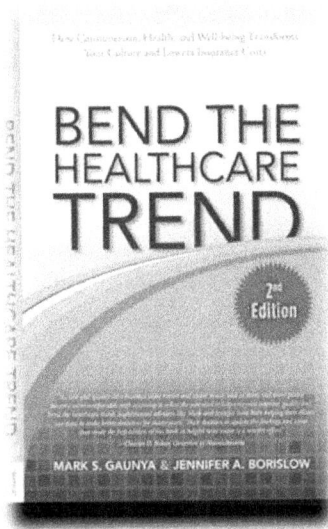

These new opportunities are now available to you and your people, and it starts with your desire to take control.

Building Literacy

The third step of the Health Insurance Hacker is when you start to settle into the new way things are working. You've taken on calculated risk and responsibility, and now that you're figuring out what is possible, you can start to operate with the confidence that you can determine the best steps to take to create the best outcomes for you and your people.

Adopting a captive self-insurance model gives you an inside look into the world of health insurance. As you begin to operate in that world—the healthcare casino, if you will—you will start to learn the language and the rules of the game. It's like figuring out how the casino functions. As you observe, you'll start to pick up on ways you might **improve your odds and lose less money**. You'll identify the games that are a money drain and the ones you have a better chance of winning. You will learn to play in such a way as to minimize loss and maximize winning.

I call this health insurance literacy. Now that you know how things work, you're not going to tolerate being denied data or being overcharged for the healthcare your people need. We talk to people all the time who don't yet know there are options besides fully insured plans. They say with assurance, "Just like death and taxes, my health insurance premiums are going to go up at least 10 percent every year." We tell them no, that's not the only option, and you don't have to settle for the less bad renewal. You can **leave the world of being unaware and enter the world of awareness and opportunity**. Once you know what possibilities are out there, you won't be blinded by the rule-making entities who designed the hamster wheel ever again.

Influencing the Outcome

We've already reviewed how the plan sponsor has fiduciary responsibility to manage all plan assets. Combining that with your newfound confidence and literacy, you have the insight and influence to create value for your people and organization. Your first priority must be to benefit your company, and there is one rule to keep in mind: **The Rule of Five.** One in every five years, your company will experience a high-cost claim year. Over the thirty-five years in this business, I can confidently tell you that's the pattern.

Underwriters do their level best to predict the financial outcome of your claims from year to year, and 95 percent of the time, they get it right. However, they get it wrong the other 5 percent of the time and don't see new emerging large claims for a variety of reasons. In health insurance, we call this large claim volatility. It's what makes CFOs uneasy because they simply don't know when it's coming. That challenging period will typically take a year or two to resolve, which is why you have to **build reserves on your balance sheet** to be able to cover those bad years when they arrive. This dynamic is also why captive self-insurance is so powerful: it allows each organization to mitigate the impact of those high-cost claims by sharing a portion of those claims with the other organizations in the risk cell, as well as the stop-loss carrier.

In the lower cost claim years, you will build reserves on your balance sheet to cover your claim liability, and you have the freedom to invest the money that has been paid into the healthcare reserves however you see fit, as long as it is in the best interests of the plan participants. As you gain confidence in understanding how the program generates cash flow, you are released from the immediate worry over monthly expenses. You can lift your sights to how your organization is performing from an overall financial perspective. Will you have a surplus this year? How much money will you receive in the form of pharmacy rebates? If either or both happen, where will you invest those dollars? If not, how much do you need to draw down on that healthcare reserve? What are you doing to help improve the health of your people, and where can those financial assets best be deployed to help them? This is a **balance sheet conversation rather than living in the operating statement.**

You can design the plan benefits the way you want. You can customize them to be exactly what your company and employees need. Remember, we don't need to stay in the realm of generalities. We can use your claim data to get specific. Do your people need better mental health support? A better pharmaceutical program? Whatever the needs are, you and your health benefits advisor can find point solutions, vet them to make sure you land on the best one, then integrate it, operationalize it, and bring it to your people.

When your people start to utilize these curated point solutions as a part of their health insurance benefits, they will become healthier, more productive, and spend less money. A healthier population means more savings for all parties, which means more money to reinvest in the health insurance plan benefits. Now, instead of asking employees for more money out of their paychecks and increasing their out-of-pocket costs, spiraling downward in the less bad renewal hamster wheel, you will start to spiral upward, saving more money and enjoying better health, all at the same time.

To make all of this value come alive and harness the power of group purchasing in a captive self-insured structure, Captivated Health has an Annual Meeting of the Membership where everyone comes together and shares how they have leveraged their literacy confidence to help their people. We get a chance to hear stories from each participating plan sponsor about what they did to help their people and the impact of those solutions on their people and bottom line.

There is one important distinction between fully-insured and captive self-insurance we have not yet talked about: **each**

year's performance stands on its own. Why is this important? In a fully-insured financing model, high-cost claim years are built into the underlying premiums that escalate from year to year, benefiting the health insurance companies in the low-cost claim years. In a captive self-insured model, each year stands on its own, which benefits the plan sponsor and plan participants.

Each year, there are winners and losers on an individual organization-by-organization level. And it is possible that even in the high-cost claim years, the shared layer (captive layer) performs favorably, and those "individual losers" mitigate their high cost claim years with captive surplus that is returned to them because the majority of the risk cell performed well. At the annual meeting, plan sponsors share stories of failures or programs that were less effective than expected. The point, however, is that they were using data to try new things, innovating, creating, and observing the impact of what they are doing. Then everyone in the community gets to benefit from the knowledge each group gains from its own experience. That is the magic of the self-governed, captive self-insured community when it is **designed like Captivated Health**.

Almost twelve years ago, the same CFOs and HR professionals on the Captivated Health Platform had no idea how to speak the language. Now, I stand back and smile as they talk about health insurance the way we do, even though it's not what they do for a living. They are fluent in the language. **Their confidence comes from understanding the game**. They now know how the healthcare casino works. They've positioned themselves in a way in which they know they can win more often than they lose. They've freed up underutilized assets to be able to add value to their employees. That's what it always comes back to: Who is benefiting? Is it the rule-making entities, or your own people and organization?

When done right, **health insurance can be an asset on the balance sheet**. Yes, it is always going to be an expense, but you'll start to save money when you take control of your plan and use data-driven analytics and targeted point solutions to mitigate your risk. Instead of that surplus going to the insurance companies, hospital systems, and drug makers, it's in the bank account of the organization for them to decide how they want to deploy it for your benefit.

These company leaders aren't going to beat the healthcare casino, but they will do a lot better than everyone who still has a blindfold on in the hamster wheel, and they have a chance to sit at the table longer.

Case Study: John's Dilemma—Too Much Money in the Healthcare Reserves

Sometimes understanding all you can do with your assets is the hardest part. John, the CFO of one of the schools in our Captivated Health Education cell, called me one day, saying, "Mark, my auditor just left. I need your help."

My immediate thought and expression to him was, "Oh boy, that does not sound like the beginning of a good conversation. What can I do to help?"

"Well, my auditors told me I have too much money saved up in my healthcare reserve account. I need to spend some of it."

I just started laughing. I told him, "You and I never used to have conversations like this when you were fully-insured. Can you please say that again!" He laughed, took a moment to reflect back on his experience, and then got a little annoyed. He said, "I am now aware that I have been getting ripped off for years, and it makes me angry. And I agree, this is genuinely a good problem to have. Can you help me?"

"But seriously, what am I supposed to do?" I suggested he lower the premium contributions he took out of people's paychecks. "No, we just did that two years ago."

"Okay," I countered, "you could contribute more money to your employees' Health Savings Accounts. You already make a generous contribution, but you could increase it."

"No, we did that last year. Sorry, Mark, you are not helping me," he said with a smile.

As part of our consulting model at Borislow Insurance, our health and well-being practice administers a survey of employees for their feedback. I looked over the results of those surveys for him and found that when we had conducted an employee interest survey at his organization, a high percentage of his employees had an interest in LASIK eye surgery. I proposed that he add that benefit to his plan as the solution to his surplus challenge.

"That won't work," he said. "LASIK isn't covered by my health insurance plan."

"It could be, though. You're in control, John," I reminded him. "All we have to do is modify your plan document (a service we provide our clients in partnership with PHIA, a highly specialized law firm that creates self-funded plan documents) and add it as a benefit. LASIK is a qualified medical expense under IRS rules. You could offer a $500 per eye benefit, or $1,000 per person. We can create a financial model for you to evaluate the cost of this solution and work out all the details."

He was thrilled to be able to add a benefit back to his plan, and his employees were able to receive a benefit tailored to their needs—a win-win-win. The situation is a great example of the value you can create when you truly understand how this all works.

7

Save Cash

Reinvest Your Dividends to
Create Greater Value

✳

W E WORKED WITH an organization once with about 600 employees down in the Boca Raton area in Florida. The ultimate goal was to help them create a culture of consumerism, health, and well-being. We began by helping them implement Health Savings Accounts (HSAs) for their employee population. They have a pretty good demographic of people who are health-conscious, so they had a good foundation to begin the journey.

We did some calculations with the CFO, and she gave us her budget target. She asked about the average rate of enrollment in organizations within the first year of offering an HSA. Implemented effectively, this strategy will create a substantially less expensive health insurance plan, so the CFO could deliver a huge positive impact on the organization's financial statement if people took advantage of the HSAs.

We shared *Bend the Healthcare Trend* with her and said if she followed that guide, our first-year average enrollment rate is 26 percent because we know how to educate people in such a way that they see the benefit of that HSA. *Bend the Healthcare Trend* is focused on this concept of getting employees engaged in their health and well-being through the health insurance plan that would benefit them most. Our unique process makes it possible to guarantee (although not explicitly) that about 26 percent of eligible people will take the HSA in the first year.

The key is to emphasize the **very strong linkage between health and wealth**. The HSA is your financial vehicle for your healthcare, and, managed properly, it can help you pay for medical expenses on a tax-preferred basis and prepare for retiree healthcare expenses as well. In fact, according to Fidelity, each of us will need to spend about $250,000 in retirement on healthcare-related expenses, so embracing HSAs helps you prepare for that financial responsibility. And the 401(k) is the financial vehicle for you to pay for living expenses in retirement. Both vehicles are interlocked. Everyone needs to prepare for their healthcare financial retirement in the same way they prepare for their overall financial retirement.

In this particular organization's case, we helped the CFO gain 42 percent of her people enrolled in the HSA during open enrollment. We almost doubled our first-year projection and helped her **save a million dollars off her budget** without sacrificing any benefits. Conversely, we added a benefit in the form of a Health Savings Account that was partially funded by the organization on behalf of its employees.

The alignment of interests between employees and their employers is critical to the positive financial performance of their health insurance plan. And done correctly, this strategy has been proven to be the real key to saving money when you join a self-insured captive. You might be fully on board, but if your plan participants don't prioritize their health, get educated, and make better, more informed decisions about their healthcare, then you can offer all the benefits in the world, and it won't do any good. The health claims from your people will continue to pile up, and the savings you experience in the captive will be diminished. It's worthwhile, then, to build our healthcare literacy and look at how to save cash after we have taken control, gained transparency, and leveraged confidence.

Engaging Your Participants

When a company is fully insured, it transfers all of its risk and control to the insurance company in exchange for a predictable monthly premium bill. Regardless of how the employer performs, the insurance company keeps those premium dollars, and as we discussed earlier, **four out of five years, they are banking all that savings**. In exchange for predictability every month about what you're being charged, you forgo the opportunity of actually spending less because your people are making smarter decisions on quality and price and, in many cases, not claiming as much as the stop-loss insurance company thinks they will.

Of course, the insurance company will try to overestimate what your people are spending so that it can make money. Say your premium was a million dollars, but you only spent $750,000. Who keeps the extra $250,000? The insurance company keeps that money on its balance sheet.

Saving money will only happen when you attack the **real driver of healthcare costs: the hidden disparity of unit costs**, which is 60 percent of the underlying price for healthcare. As an example, say you need to get an MRI, and you have two options of equal quality. However, one of those diagnostic tests is delivered in a hospital, and the other is in a free-standing facility that only does MRIs. Both places would administer the procedure through a person with the same level of education. One of them costs $500, and the other is $5,000.

Why the disparity? There's no reason somebody should pay $4,500 more for the same service, so what is driving that price difference?

As the person in need of the MRI, let's say you have a $50 copay regardless of where you go for that service. More than likely, you're going to choose the $5,000 MRI because there is a universal understanding that if something costs more, it's usually associated with higher quality. You care less about the cost, and you don't know (because no one told you) that there is little to no difference in quality.

However, if you were enrolled in a Health Savings Account and exposed to the true total cost of the service, and **if your company offered you an incentive** to make a less expensive choice, perhaps you would choose the $500 MRI in this situation. You'd be rewarded with $250 from your employer and enjoy a better experience than if you went to the hospital, considering this location specializes entirely in MRIs. What's more, you're saving your employer money, which shows up in lower employee premium contributions from your paycheck. **Today's claims are always tomorrow's premium.**

This is only one example of price disparity. It happens with prescription drugs, surgery, hospitalization, or anything else involved in healthcare. In fact, there are roughly 330 areas of healthcare where consumers can make a choice and a better decision.

We're not talking about life-threatening illnesses like cancer or emergency situations. If I get in a car accident, I'm not going to be pulling out my phone to look up which hospital will be less expensive. Price should never factor into a time-sensitive emergency like that.

Filtering out those infrequent experiences, we're left with the predictable, like CAT scans, MRIs, x-rays, blood work, prescription drugs, or elective outpatient surgery. People have an opportunity to make an informed choice about these services when they have information and support available to them. However, we ask again, if the consumer is paying the same amount no matter what choice they make, is there any reason to choose thoughtfully? The simple answer is no.

This is where the structure of being a self-insured organization can help you implement the right incentives for your people to make good choices when it comes to their healthcare. Think of it this way: **you, the employer, save money—you win—when your employees make smart, quality, and cost-conscious decisions**. What are you going to do with those savings? Going back to the MRI example, you would save $4,500 every time someone chooses the $500 option. If you share just 10 percent of those savings with your employee, you'd be saving about $4,000 instead. We call this a **shared savings model**. That's still an incredible win, and now you get to share the win with your employee as a thank you for making smart choices.

The core principle built into the foundation of Captivated Health is to serve the individual member—the plan participant. As such, we don't believe in telling anybody what to do with their healthcare. What we will do, however, is offer solutions that benefit all parties. If an organization has a situation, informed by the data we've talked about, we're reaching out with the information to assist the employee through a clinical concierge service. Or the member can reach out to the concierge service, tell them what is needed, and then the service will provide informed choices that are unique to that individual. The bottom line, however, is that those choices are yours to make. They are your employees' choices to make. The way it should be.

Remember the story I told at the very beginning about Harpeth Hall's maternity program offering free diapers and wipes for a year? That's a perfect example of the type of incentive we're talking about. You don't have to enroll in the maternity program if you're expecting. But if you do, you will receive all the benefits Harpeth Hall has negotiated on your behalf, including free diapers and wipes and dedicated care for twelve months. **Everyone wins when you opt in.**

This step must come last in the Health Insurance Hacker because it builds on the literacy component. If an employee doesn't know how to access healthcare intelligently, three things will happen. They will get poor-quality care. They will get more expensive care. And they will get frustrated with the process. But when you can help them make informed decisions, support them through those decisions, and reward them for making the right ones, everyone benefits.

People don't want a convincing argument. They want a compelling offer. You can create the best health insurance plan the world has ever seen, but if your employees don't care about it personally, then it's not an asset; it's just an expense. It's just another liability on your balance sheet. As soon as you start offering data-driven solutions that address specific needs and properly incentivize participation, you've unlocked the secret to taking control of your health insurance and improving your odds in the healthcare casino.

Case Study: Michael S. Komich, Senior Vice President for Finance and Operations at Cheverus High School (Portland, ME), in his own words, on getting his employees engaged in their health and wellbeing

Cheverus High School in Portland, Maine, is a college Jesuit preparatory school, grades 9 through 12, boys and girls, day only. I have just completed my thirty-fifth year with the school, and we joined Captivated Health in year two of its conception. We came to the captive from a fully insured financing structure for our health insurance plan. We examined Captivated Health as a way of continuing excellent health insurance for our employees and their tethered family members, but trying to also leverage the cost outcomes of health insurance. Health insurance had taken a pretty prominent spot on our budget. At about half a million dollars annually, we thought it was a big number that maybe we could do something about.

We were told to expect about a million dollars of savings over five years when we switched, and the projection landed true. Fast forward to the present, we have a soft landing spot annually of between $250,000 and $275,000, and that's all in (claims, premiums, fees, and wellness programs). We have added more benefits, which is beyond what we used to do when we were fully insured, and the options were to raise per paycheck premiums or increase deductibles.

Because of our savings, we are able to offer a variety of choices for our employees. They can choose between a health savings account or a health reimbursement account. We also frontload the first dollar coverage of each employee's plan with either $900 of employer funding toward the annual deductible for a single adult, or $1,875 for a two-person family deductible. In addition, we offer wellness benefits where an employee can do a few things to lower the cost of their health insurance plan even further.

They can submit to biometric screening, cholesterol tests, height, weight, and body fat analyses, and micro health coaching sessions. These **health-conscious choices** will save them 10 percent of their premium per paycheck contributions if they couple it with a health risk assessment online. It is entirely **optional**, of course, but the offer incentivizes our employees to be conscious about their health. We offer various other paycheck benefits as well when our employees engage in a virtual visit with a service provider, register their maintenance prescriptions for mail order delivery, engage the services of a health guide to source care from a service provider, research or receive cost and quality of care analyses on their healthcare service decisions, or participate in an employer-funded patient relationship with a choice of two Direct Primary Care (DPC) physicians.

All of this is intended to create an attitude with our employees to pursue excellent healthcare for themselves or their family while being aware of the consumerism tied to today's healthcare system. Every informed decision our employees make affects us positively. We just received our numbers for the current year, and **our health insurance costs are going down again**, like they do every year, despite having high-cost claimants. In the last five years, our average annual increase has been **only 3.5 percent**, which is very close to inflation and very acceptable when it comes to health insurance cost increases.

That's the strength of the Captivated Health Platform. We have twenty-nine members this year in our captive cell, and every school that joins shares a level of risk with other schools and helps blunt the catastrophic claims before they even get to the stop-loss carrier's doorstep. **It is truly an effective health insurance financing model.**

Case Study: Marge Pierce, Former CFO of Tower School in Marblehead, Massachusetts, in her own words, on flexibility with control

Tower School joined Captivated Health in its second year of operation. When I came into the school as the director of finance and operations, I didn't know a thing about self-funded health insurance, so my first year was a crash course in understanding how everything worked and what the benefits were. As I gained understanding, I realized how beneficial it was to both the school and the employees.

This is such an **incredible opportunity for a school to manage health insurance costs**. At the same time, it provides a chance to share with employees how to be healthy and to encourage a healthy lifestyle. The whole model of Captivated Health is for people to be healthy. The school does better when the employees are healthy. But also, it's such a benefit to the employees to be able to take advantage of different resources available to help them pay attention to their health and be a better consumer.

The downside of self-funding your health insurance, especially for such a small school, is that there is additional work involved—it's a participatory model. We had a business office of two, so trying to do all of the things that a regular business office does and run a self-insured plan at the same time was tricky. But we had incredible support from Captivated Health, and we had the flexibility to offer our employees some incentives. We signed up for Rightway and encouraged people to get the app and use it to research all their healthcare needs and questions.

We also offered small lifestyle bonuses, like credit for joining a gym. Even with a small budget and a small team, we found ways to promote employee health within our plan.

The flexibility was everything. When a faculty member's child had a serious accident, our plan covered the emergency care, but then the child needed physical therapy. Because the child was away at college, their physical therapy would not have been covered. We were able to amend our plan document in order to get the coverage they needed. In moments like that, there is so much panic about how terrible the situation is, but it is also a good reminder that people need to pay attention to what their plan covers. In Captivated Health, if the coverage needs to change, it's always a possibility.

Because we are grouped with like-minded schools, CFOs, and HR managers, we can get together every year and discuss our individual and collective performance. It's a useful discussion, and everyone is willing to listen to and discuss others' ideas. I appreciate not being dictated to. I get to share my input, identify problems, and try to make a change.

Every institution has to do their own due diligence when it comes to self-insuring your health insurance plan. It is not right for everyone, and a lot depends on how sensitive your budget is. If you have the opportunity, as we did at Tower, to build up a reserve, that is the ideal way to go. Because then, when you do inevitably have those tough years, you're not paying extra out of tuition that you collected that year. You have slowly put a little bit away to manage those inevitable hard years.

8

Human-Level Impact

❋

WE HAVE SEEN several examples of the benefits that Captivated Health can provide via the Health Insurance Hacker, including incredible freedom of cash flow, control over your plan, and visibility like you've never had before. And there is one benefit that forms the backbone of the Hack: **enabling employers to better care for their people**.

Healthcare should have an overall positive effect on people. However, I have seen case after case of people who are fed up, impoverished, or scarred by their experience with the current system. This is one reason I co-created the **NABIP Healthcare Consumer Bill of Rights**.[9] Since 2005, I have been a member of an employee benefits professional association called NABIP, the National Association of Benefits and Insurance Professionals. In an effort to **lift the conversation out of politics and into sound public policy**, we developed ten rights (principles) that any one of us would want as a healthcare consumer:

---

[9]   https://nabip.org/media/9257/nabip-healthcare-bill-of-rights-final.pdf

◯ NABIP American Healthcare Consumer Bill of Rights

Preamble

We, the people of the United States, recognizing the importance of access to affordable high-quality healthcare, hereby establish this American Healthcare Consumer Bill of Rights. It is our fundamental belief that every individual deserves the right to obtain healthcare that is comprehensive, equitable, and compassionate. This bill serves to protect and uphold these rights for all Americans.

Article I: Right to Access Affordable Healthcare
1. Every American shall have the right to access affordable healthcare that meets the consumer's needs, regardless of age, gender, race, ethnicity, socioeconomic status, or pre-existing conditions.
2. The healthcare sector shall strive to ensure that essential healthcare services, including preventive care, medical treatments, medications, mental health and substance abuse disorder services, are accessible and affordable for all individuals.

Article II: Right to Quality Care
1. When accessing healthcare, every American shall expect to receive quality healthcare services that meet or exceed established standards of care that are transparent and clinically appropriate.
2. Healthcare providers and institutions shall be held accountable for maintaining the highest levels of quality, safety, and efficacy in their practices.

Article III: Right to Privacy and Confidentiality
1. Every American shall have the right to privacy and confidentiality in all health-care-related matters.
2. Healthcare providers and institutions shall protect the privacy and confidentiality of patients' medical information, adhering to strict standards and regulations.

Article IV: Right to Informed Autonomy
1. Every American shall have the right to make informed decisions regarding their healthcare, including the right to refuse or consent to medical treatment.
2. Healthcare providers shall respect and honor the autonomy of patients, providing them with all relevant information to make informed decisions about their health.

Article V: Right to Health Equity
1. Every American shall have the right to healthcare that is equitably, just, and free from discrimination.
2. The healthcare sector shall take necessary measures to address and eliminate health disparities, ensuring that underserved populations have equal access to healthcare resources and services.
3. Every assessment of social determinants of health, including economic stability, education access and quality, neighborhood and physical infrastructure, social and community context.

Article VI: Right to Health Education
1. Every American shall have the right to access comprehensive health education and information to promote personal well-being and prevention of diseases.
2. The healthcare sector shall prioritize health education programs, including public health campaigns, to empower individuals with the knowledge to make informed decisions about their health.

Article VII: Right to Affordable Medications
1. Every American shall have the right to access affordable medications necessary for their health and well-being.
2. The healthcare sector shall implement policies to ensure the affordability and availability of essential medications, including the oversight and transparency of drug prices and the promotion of generic/biosimilar alternatives.

Article VIII: Right to Emergency Care
1. Every American shall have the right to emergency medical care without fear of financial hardship.
2. Healthcare providers shall be obligated to provide emergency care to all individuals in need, regardless of their ability to pay, ensuring that no one is denied life-saving treatment due to financial constraints.

Article IX: Right to Healthcare Advocacy
1. Every American shall have the right to an effective and accessible healthcare advocacy system.
2. Every American shall have the right to complain, refer concerns, grievances and pursue expedited appeal of coverage determinations.
3. The government shall establish mechanisms for individuals to seek assistance and resolve grievances related to their healthcare, ensuring that their rights are protected and upheld.

Article X: State Rights
1. Consumers access healthcare and insurance markets locally.
2. Each state regulates the healthcare and insurance markets and is charged with protecting the consumer.
3. States will embody these principles of consumer protection and be permitted to have oversight within the healthcare eco-system within its state borders, except to compete for eligible or private healthcare market.

Conclusion
The NABIP American Healthcare Consumer Bill of Rights serves as a guiding framework to ensure that healthcare remains primarily accessible and affordable for all Americans. It is a commitment to promoting health, dignity, and equality, and it is the responsibility of all individuals and the healthcare sector to uphold and protect these rights.

◯ NABIP

- The Right to Access Affordable Healthcare
- The Right to High-Quality Healthcare
- The Right to Privacy and Confidentiality
- The Right to Individual Autonomy
- The Right to Health Equity
- The Right to Health Education
- The Right to Affordable Medications
- The Right to Emergency Care
- The Right to Health Advocacy
- States Rights

These principles form the ten articles we uphold in order to protect the consumer when it comes to their healthcare. They are essential to guide discussions around healthcare policy changes. We look at every proposed policy change through the lens of the Healthcare Consumer Bill of Rights. Even if the proposal is well-intentioned, it must support the Articles in order to be supported by our association. Best of all, because

NABIP

Consumer Bill of Rights Scorecard

Professionals - Shaping the Future of Healthcare (Page 1)   Name: Delta Force   Date: February 14, 2024

Mindsets	1	2	3	4	5	6	7	8	9	10	11	12
Right to Access Affordable Healthcare	Americans have poor access to affordable healthcare based on their socio-economic position, diverse needs and the healthcare sector doesn't their individual desires		Americans have limited access to affordable healthcare based on their socio-economic position, diverse needs and the healthcare sector restricts their individual desires			Americans have reasonable access to affordable healthcare based on their socio-economic position, diverse needs and the healthcare sector restricts their individual desires			Americans have access to affordable healthcare that meets their needs for preventive care, medical treatments, medications, mental health and substance abuse disorder services			
Right to High Quality Healthcare	Americans receive sub-standard quality healthcare with little to no transparency and healthcare providers are not held accountable		Americans receive average quality healthcare with little transparency and some healthcare providers are held accountable			Americans receive above average quality healthcare with some transparency and most healthcare providers are held accountable			Americans receive high quality healthcare services that exceed quality and transparency standards and all healthcare providers are held accountable to that high standard			
Right to Privacy & Confidentiality	Americans right to privacy and confidentiality of their healthcare is not protected and providers and institutions are not held accountable for maintaining that privacy standard		Americans right to privacy and confidentiality of their healthcare is somewhat protected and providers and institutions are not held accountable for that privacy			Americans right to privacy and confidentiality of their healthcare is somewhat protected and some providers and institutions are held accountable to that privacy			Americans have a right to privacy and confidentiality of their healthcare and providers and institutions protect the privacy and confidentiality of all consumers medical information			
Right to individual Autonomy	Americans are not informed about their healthcare choices and receive no guidance. Healthcare system withholds information and restricts choices		Americans are somewhat informed about their healthcare choices and often receive information and guidance. Healthcare system restricts information and choices			Americans are mostly informed about their healthcare choices and given information and guidance. Healthcare system sometimes limits information and choices			Americans have a right to make decisions about their healthcare, including refusal of treatment and system honor individual choice and freedom of information to inform			
Right to Health Equity	Americans experience negative social determinants of health, have poor access to HC, experience economic and cultural bias and have limited access to education		Americans experience some negative social determinants of health, some access to HC, some economic and cultural bias and some access to education			Americans experience lower number of negative social determinants of health, greater access to HC, less economic and cultural bias and more access to education			Americans have a right to healthcare that is equitable and free from discrimination and the system eliminates disparities and creates awareness of social determinants			
Right to Health Education	Americans are uneducated about their rights to information to help them prevent disease and general well-being and the system makes no efforts to educate and inform		Americans have some access to health education and information; the HC sector provides generalized health education platforms with limited community programs			Americans have improved access to health education and information; the HC sector provides some targeted health education programs through extensive benefits			Americans have a right to education that promotes personal well-being, disease prevention and system engages and empowers consumers through health campaigns			
Right to Affordable Medications	Americans access to affordable medications is restricted and the system provides little to no transparency about prices or the availability of lower cost options		Americans have access to some affordable preventive generic medications; the HC sector prevents easy access to pricing transparency and promotion of lower cost options			Americans have improved access to affordable preventive generic medications; the HC sector provides access to pricing transparency tools and promotes lower cost options			Americans have a right to access medications for health and wellbeing and the system creates policies that provide transparency of drug prices and promotes lower cost options			
Right to Emergency Care	Americans are unaware of their right to emergency healthcare and avoid treatment due to financial constraints		Americans have limited knowledge of their right to access to emergency care, uninformed about their financial			Americans have improved access to emergency HC, informed about their right to emergency HC and			Americans have a right to emergency healthcare without fear of financial hardship and the system			

we developed a Scorecard, we can score every proposal and provide specific areas where the recommended policy change must improve to be supported by NABIP.

To access a complete version of this Scorecard, scan the following QR code.

With these principles in place, we are removing the political biases and motives from every conversation. It's not about an agenda. It's about what is in the best interest of the consumer. Instead of saying, I'm a Republican, I'm a Democrat, I'm an Independent, we steer the conversation to the principles we stand for.

The Captivated Health Platform was built with these same principles in mind, even though their formal creation wasn't until years later. **It's all about making the consumer's experience as positive as possible and one that protects their rights**. These principles can also be applied to the fiduciary role of a plan sponsor and ensure that the employer (plan sponsor) is fulfilling their responsibility to continually improve the value of the health insurance plan for the participants. To that end, let's look at a few more case studies and examples of the impact Captivated Health has had on the individual employers and their health insurance plans.

"In The Red" with Financial Feasibility, Green Lights with Mindset and Risk Tolerance

Generally, the best time to transition from a fully-insured to a self-insured financing plan is when coming off a year with a modest fully-insured renewal rate increase. However, there are certainly exceptions, which we've proven through several experiences. One was with a school in northern New England that began investigating Captivated Health after absorbing multiple double-digit renewals. They were once again facing a 20 percent increase on their fully insured plan.

We helped them determine that most of the adverse claim activity was due to a small group of faculty and staff. That small bit of information opened the door to believing the increases were manageable with a thoughtful plan. Although the initial Captivated Health feasibility analysis came in at a 30 percent increase, the **CFO took the risk head-on**, assured that this would be a long-term solution providing control, stability, and savings. And **she was right**.

The first step was for the school to gain access to its data. Captivated Health worked with them to analyze their information and devise strategies for mitigating the worst of the claims. Management decided to use the data to provide transparency to the faculty and staff, enabling them to make intelligent healthcare choices. The school also implemented a multi-year health and well-being strategy encompassing physical, financial, workplace, community, and mind and spirit components to support the overall lives of faculty and staff.

The results? In year one, **the plan built up a reserve** of $269,000 as a hedge against future claims. In year two, the plan **only increased 6.4 percent**, allowing the school to keep employee and staff contributions unchanged. The reserve fund increased by $110,000. In year three, the school achieved the predictability and stability they were after. With another favorable renewal, there was **again no contribution increase or watering down of plan benefits**.

Even with a challenging first-year financial feasibility, the right mindset, proper planning, transparency, and an emphasis on holistic well-being resulted in a favorable environment for all involved.

Cheryl York, Director of Finance and HR at Erskine Academy, in her own words, about leveraging the law of large numbers to create scale

One of the things I most appreciate about the Captivated Health team is that they will let you know if you aren't ready to make the switch to a self-insured plan. We didn't immediately switch to the Captivated Health Platform when we were introduced to it because we were not yet in the right financial place to make it a good fit. Mark and the team monitored our progress, **advising us exactly when it would most benefit us** to make the switch.

We were at the point where we had a total of a 36 percent increase over the course of three consecutive years. We were paying the high health insurance premiums with no end in sight. If the premiums weren't used, the money was gone; nothing came back to the school. It was time to find a better solution.

As we learned about Captivated Health, **the most attractive aspect was the spread of the risk.** We're a small school with only about eighty-five employees, so we would never be able to self-insure on our own. When grouped with other schools, we were afforded an opportunity we never could have had otherwise.

I felt, as I'm sure many school administrators and business officers do, spread too thin to be able to fully educate myself in the health insurance world. The **benefit of Captivated**

Health was that they brought their experience and expertise and gave me the tools I needed to be able to feel confident with this transition. When everything was laid out in terms of the potential cost savings, there was not much deliberation from our headmaster or the board. It was clear this was the next step for the school.

My family is now enrolled in our benefit package here. If you have an appointment scheduled, the concierge does research for you to determine whether you can go to a less expensive facility for the same care and save the school that money. My husband had an endoscopy scheduled at a local hospital, but when we called the concierge to shop around for us, they found a better alternative. It was a forty-minute drive away, but the price difference was so significant that he could save $250. We easily agreed that a slightly longer drive was well worth the savings.

Captivated Health provided us opportunities like this to allow for significant cost savings while providing the same, if not better, care, options, and benefits for our employees. As a finance and HR manager, I particularly appreciate that we get to give more ownership to employees to make better healthcare decisions for themselves. It **builds trust in the joint relationship** because they know the school is working for them.

Dean Sidell, Director of Finance and Operations at the Landmark School, in his own words, giving us the best of both worlds: ROI and ROE

Landmark is a private, independent school that has two campuses, one in Beverly, Massachusetts, and the other in Manchester by the Sea. We are a school of 480 students serving high-aptitude, high-IQ, language-based learning differences. We have both a day and a boarding program, and we have about 320 employees.

Landmark is actually the second school I introduced to Captivated Health. The first school I joined through was the Tower School (still in the cell under different leadership), where we were with Captivated Health for almost ten years. When I came to Landmark, we once again looked at Captivated Health and compared it to the other options in the market and determined it was by far the **best option for the school's finances and the benefits it brings our employees**.

For years, we in the independent school world struggled to find ways to manage our health insurance premiums. **Things were done to us instead of for us or by us**. There was no real management opportunity. The captive financing structure gives us the ability to help manage and enhance the benefits for our employees and lower costs.

For their part, our employees love the plan. They love that we are able to structure the plan design benefits in such a way that it will work for them. We can add benefits based on school needs, and we get to provide services a traditional health insurance plan might not provide.

Once we were onboarded into Captivated Health, we started to build financial reserves. Whenever we had a year where our claims were less than our claim projections, we got to keep those dollars on the school's balance sheet. We could then invest the surplus in other benefits for the plan participants. The Captivated Health eco-system gives us stability in the world of health insurance premium rollercoasters—what Mark calls the hamster wheel of less bad renewals.

The other benefit is that we receive reports on our data. They are non-specific person reports, not tied to a specific employee or their family members. We get data on what is being used within our plan. Are people going to the doctor for their wellness visits? Are they getting care for this condition or that? Are they using the prescription drug plan? And if so, for what? Are they utilizing the resources we have provided?

Based on the answers to these questions, we can direct education toward the need and provide solutions that target the things our people are actually dealing with. For example, after recognizing a general need for mental health support among the children of our staff and faculty, we were able to provide services to help. Similarly, because we are located in Boston, we have some of the best cancer treatment facilities and doctors in the world. We've been able to help people get the best care. **The gratitude we receive from those who have benefited is enough to make it worthwhile. It's Return on Investment for the school and Return on Experience for our people.**

The key to it all has been getting employees to participate. We understand that we have to incentivize our people to do the right thing, even when they know it. One way we have accomplished this is through per paycheck contributions to their Health Savings Account (HSA). Essentially, we tell them we can't make healthcare choices on their behalf, but we can give them high-quality, cost-efficient ways to do it better, then reward good choices with our HSA contributions.

Captivated Health **gives us the best of both worlds**. It gives us a group dynamic where we are sharing a certain amount of risk with other like-minded schools with similar risk profiles to our own. We're sharing risk with other schools that understand our risk cell. And the risk factors are similar to those in a fully insured financing structure. You're going to pay for health claims regardless, so you might as well **find a better way to manage those claims** that allows you to save money whenever possible.

Kathleen Howe, Director of Finance and Operations at New Hampton School & Joe Williams, Head of School at New Hampton, in their own words, about the acceleration of consumerism

New Hampton School was the first founding member school in the Captivated Health Education cell. It was brand new. The health insurance renewal scene was a black abyss and lacked any valuable information. Each year, we would get a health insurance premium increase with no explanation. We got an invoice, but that's it. There wasn't any exchange of information or transparency. We had no clue how much of our money was actually going towards paying our claims. We decided to use the situation as an opportunity to explore our options and the captive financing structure.

Being so early to the platform, we didn't have examples to follow. We were ready to take the calculated risks, and we didn't go in without vetting the decision. We crunched numbers and made all the observations we could, even conducted round-table education meetings with a cross-section of our faculty and staff. Our goal was to launch it as effectively as possible with as little disruption to employees as possible.

In the early years, the transition was complicated from a finance aspect, but to the end users—our employees—nothing changed too drastically. The real difference was that we started talking about consumerism. When someone asked why certain prices were so high or complained about not understanding their claims and deductible expenses, we could sit down with them and answer questions. Instead of the abyss of nothingness, **we had information and data like we'd never known before.**

ver the eleven years we've been on the platform, we have had some years with higher claims exposure, but recently every year has been in the single digits. When our claims projections are higher than expected, the **increase has only been 2 or 3 percent,** well below inflation.

Our employees have expressed a high level of confidence that the school is working in their best interests. The Captivated Health Platform gives us more choice as to how we support our employees. We have tried a few options when it comes to incentive programs, and some have worked better than others. Initially, we built in a per-paycheck premium contribution reduction incentive plan, but it didn't feel right for us. We had to ask our employees for proof of their tests, procedures, and appointments, and we felt it was too invasive.

What did work was our current wellness benefit reimbursement program. Up to a certain dollar amount, we reimburse our employees for their health-conscious purchases, like a gym membership or a kayak. That has been popular and well-utilized.

One of the things to come out of Captivated Health is the boost to consumerism. We have folks now who understand that they can pick up the phone and ask how much a service is going to cost them. Instead of being faced with blank screens and an ambiguous bill, they can access information about price and quality. Most importantly, they know it's their right to ask for that information, and we provide the support they need through the concierge.

We love the Captivated Health design from an administrative point of view because it is so collaborative. Independent schools tend to be a collaborative bunch, so this health insurance model fits well with our thinking. If we are having trouble with something, we can reach out to peers in the captive to see if they are having similar issues. Or if we have a new financial controller, for example, our peer schools are more than happy to have their financial controller help train that person from their own experience. **Members look after members.**

There's a degree of internal collaboration as well that Captivated Health requires to work well. Employees are educated on how they can save individually, but also on how they are helping their colleagues when they collectively make choices that reduce expenses for the whole school. It's a healthy model that I wish we could expand to work in other areas of our operation.

For anyone considering joining Captivated Health, remember to foster this collaborative spirit from the start. You have to **get buy-in from your employees at a high level**. They don't need to understand all the logistical details about captive self-insurance, reinsurance, or stop-loss coverage—their eyes will glaze over. If all they understand to start with is the transparency and information exchange that will be available to them, it's often enough to get everyone on board and excited about a **health insurance platform that truly benefits everyone involved.**

Bob Kramer, Assistant Head for Finance and Operations at Lawrence Academy, in his own words, about taking control and assuming responsibility

I've been at Lawrence for ten years now after a thirty-year career in investment management, sales, and trading. The transition to the nonprofit space was a career pivot, but it gave me a refreshing perspective on my work life. I was used to being surrounded twenty-four-seven by people whose sole concern was making money. Now to be in an environment where the top priority is adding value to people's lives, the change was dramatic. It gave me perspective on what employee benefits really mean. Particularly in a boarding school environment, where we provide housing and meals and a community for their children to go to school, it's crucial to get employee benefits right.

Our community at Lawrence is a fishbowl in some ways—everyone knows what's going on with everyone else. So when someone has healthcare problems, everyone has a pretty good sense of whether it's taken care of in an excellent way. **Captivated Health has been our answer for ensuring every person receives excellent care.**

The first benefit I noticed when we switched to Captivated Health was **the control that came with taking responsibility for our health insurance**. When we were fully insured, we transferred all risk to the third party (health insurance company). We know to some extent that our performance was going to affect our renewal costs, but the connection didn't feel very direct. Renewal costs were going to go up no matter what we did. After the switch, we could no longer make our health claims risk someone else's problem. We had to start taking accountability for how much we spent, where those dollars were going, and what the results looked like.

Just by paying attention, we noticed a discrepancy between what we budgeted for health insurance and what our actual claims were. We have to realize all those savings and start building a reserve on our balance sheet instead of blindly allowing a third party to take the profit. That reserve has been crucial for providing a cushion. We are able to shoulder more risk without passing it on to our employees.

When we first introduced the concept of partially self-insured health insurance to our employees, a few people were hesitant, afraid that the new model would force them to feel guilty for getting sick because of the impact on cost. We explained that everything worked the same way—**nothing was free before, and it wasn't free now**—but that this new model allowed for partnership between employee and employer in navigating the system and making educated healthcare decisions that lead to lower costs. Incentive programs help align the employee with that collaboration mentality.

People will spend hours researching the best flatscreen TV to buy, then spend three more hours telling the tale of the top-rated TV they found and how it's being delivered and set up for them. But the same person could have just spent five times as much money on a shoulder surgery without ever realizing a less expensive and more effective professional than the one they saw was available. When it comes to health, we have been unwilling to do the same research we do with everything else, partly because of the lack of available information.

At one time, I was dealing with some shoulder pain, so I went to see my primary care physician. He put me through some movements and determined that I likely had a small tear in my rotator cuff. After sending me for an X-ray to verify, he told me that at my age, I was not a good candidate for rotator cuff surgery. Instead, he recommended physical therapy for a gradual recovery. Many physicians would have sent me straight to an orthopedic surgeon who would have done the surgery without a second thought, but because my primary care doctor was willing to be transparent with me, I was able to make a smart decision for myself in my stage of life and avoid the surgery. Through Captivated Health, all of our members are able to make informed decisions about their healthcare, and when they do, **they get better care, and we all pay lower prices.**

9

Captivated Health Scorecard

Mindset and Risk Profile

✹

N
OW THAT YOU know how the Hack works, it's time to start considering how the Hack could work for you and your organization. Captivated Health is not a solution for every organization. It was designed for the RIGHT organizations, determined by mindset and suitability (risk profile). To make that design more understandable, we've put together a Scorecard with a set of attributes, each accompanied by the ideal mindset a Captivated Health member organization must embrace in order to gain access to the platform. This is one way we assess who would be a right fit for joining. We look at an organization's ranking in these areas:

COMMUNITY ASSESSMENT

Captivated Health — PROSPECTIVE CAPTIVE MEMBER EVALUATION — Name — Date

Text	1	2	3	4	5	6	7	8	9	10	11	12	Score
1 DECISION MAKING	C-suite has no involvement in the decision-making process. All benefits decisions are made with the HR team.			C-suite has little involvement in the decision-making process. HR reports benefits decisions to the C-suite for final approval.			C-suite is involved in the decision-making process, but views cost increases as inevitable.			C-suite is heavily involved and views controlling health insurance costs as a major organizational priority.			
2 BENEFIT PHILOSOPHY ALIGNMENT	We offer benefits because we have to, not because we choose to.			We offer benefits because we choose to, but only want to deal with it once a year.			Providing benefits is important, but we tend to push cost increases to our employees through reduced coverage and/or increased premium contributions.			Providing benefits is integral to the success of our organization and is key to attracting and retaining talent.			
3 RISK PROFILE	We prefer to let the carrier take all of the risk even if it means we are paying more and have little control.			We would be willing to take some risk but have been told that partial self-funding will give us too much financial exposure.			We are willing to assume some risk but just don't know enough about partial self-funding to make the move.			We are willing to assume risk and see self-funding as an opportunity to control/reduce our health insurance costs.			
4 FINANCIAL SUITABILITY	Monthly cash flow is a big concern. We are struggling financially.			Overall, our organization is financially stable, but cash flow is still a major concern.			We are financially stable but a market shift would have a significant impact on our cash flow			Our organization is financially sound and cash flow is not a concern			
5 GROUP SIZE	Fewer than 50 employees			50-75 employees			75-99 employees			More than 100 employees			
6 RENEWAL HISTORY	Over the past 2-3 years, our average health insurance renewal increase has been 20% or more (not including plan changes).			Over the past 2-3 years, our average health insurance renewal increase has been 15-20% (not including plan changes)			Over the past 2-3 years, our average health insurance renewal increase has been 10-15% (not including plan changes)			Over the past 2-3 years, our average health insurance renewal increase has been less than 10% (not including plan changes).			
7 BENEFIT EDUCATION AND COMMUNICATION	Benefit education and communication is only needed when plan changes occur.			We provide benefit education and communication once a year at open enrollment.			We provide benefit education and communication more than once a year but don't want to burden employees with too much information.			We provide ongoing, year-round benefit education and communication. We believe it is vital to our long-term success.			
8 RISK MANAGEMENT	We don't like to get involved with our employees' health. It is too invasive.			We care about our employees' health but, let's be honest - it doesn't impact our insurance costs.			We believe in managing risk, but know that we can't improve our efforts.			We understand that our health insurance costs are a direct result of the decisions our employees make. Therefore, risk mitigation is imperative.			
Scorecard	→ → → →			⇒ ⇒ ⇒ ⇒			⇒ ⇒ ⇒			⇒ ⇒ ⇒ ⇒			

- Decision-Making
- Benefit Philosophy Alignment
- Risk Profile
- Financial Suitability
- Group Size
- Renewal History
- Benefit Education and Communication
- Risk Management

As we dive into each of these attributes, we consider how well you and your organization align with the ideal mindset. If you identify with some of those attributes and experience less alignment with others, we make a note of those areas for deeper exploration.

To download your own Community Assessment Scorecard, visit CaptivatedHealth.com/Book or scan the following QR code.

Decision-Making

When we talk about decision-making, we're looking at how involved the C-suite and executive leadership are currently in the health insurance offering for their company. The ideal organization has a **heavily invested C-suite**. These leaders understand that their benefits line is the second largest expense on their operating statement, and they prioritize that line item in their strategic plan. Some organizations don't do that. They have other competing priorities, so they leave it entirely to the HR team to handle. Even if they know they are wasting money every year on their health insurance plan, it's not enough of a priority for them to directly intervene. The right mindset C-suite is frustrated with the hamster wheel, and they are willing to take control in order to lead their organization off that hamster wheel and the less bad renewal.

Take a moment to consider where you fall along this continuum. Is your executive leadership involved? Do they instead hand over the responsibility to their HR team? Is optimizing the health insurance plan performance a major organizational priority?

Benefit Philosophy Alignment

The major question to ask here is one of motive. Why do you provide benefits to your employees? Is it because you are required to, or because you choose to? Do you value benefits as part of the overall compensation package to retain and attract talent? If you find yourself viewing benefits as merely a necessary expense, then it will be much more difficult to have success in a self-insured captive. **Captive members must take an active approach** in crafting their health plan design and benefits in order to create a mutually constructive relationship between the employer and employees. And **getting your employees engaged is the single biggest challenge and opportunity.** If you view benefits as an integral component to the success of your organization or as the key to attracting and retaining talent, then a self-insured captive solution might be the next step for you.

Risk Profile

When we're assessing whether an employer is the right type of organization to join a Captivated Health risk cell, we look at two things within their risk profile. First, they have to be willing risk-takers with high risk tolerance. And they must be suitable to take that risk, meaning their risk profile is appropriate to be self-insured. They must see being self-insured as an opportunity to control the uncontrollable and proactively implement solutions to the real challenges of their employees. For someone risk-averse, on the other hand, it doesn't matter whether the best counsel advises them to take a risk; an overabundance of caution will hold them back.

Caution certainly has its place in a self-insured captive, but if you're not willing to take any risk, a captive solution is not going to work for you. Taking smart, informed risks opens the door to reducing health insurance costs and improving the overall value for employees.

Financial Suitability

Many organizations we talk to would love to be in a self-insured captive. They check all the other boxes but don't have enough cash flow in their business to substantiate the responsibility that being a self-funded plan sponsor requires. The truth is you must have enough money on the balance sheet to be able to pay the claims when they materialize, as you will not be transferring all your risk to an insurance company. In a self-insured captive, you can share in some of the risk due to the nature of the captive structure, but you must have enough liquidity to handle your share. Ideally, cash flow should not be a big concern for your organization.

Group Size

The ideal size of a Captivated Health employer is roughly 50 enrolled employees to 500 employees. As a rule of thumb, we don't offer captive self-insurance to employers with less than 50 enrolled. The reason is that stop-loss carriers can't collect enough stop-loss premium to cover the large claim risk, and the other participating captive members assume a lot of the risk associated with that smaller employer. All it takes is one or two large claims, and the employer hasn't paid enough reinsurance premium to cover the exposure to the stop-loss carrier, and they take more money out of the captive layer than what they paid in.

These are straightforward criteria that most stop-loss carriers are reluctant to change.

Renewal History

If we come across an employer that has received a rate increase of over 20 percent over the past few years, that tells us and the stop-loss underwriters a few things. Most likely, they have had those consistent double-digit rate increases because the underlying risk of the group is not favorable. One large increase might not indicate the same thing (see the rule of five), but when the annual renewal increase average remains high for multiple years, that group is most likely not a good candidate to be self-insured. In fact, being fully insured tends to be the best option for those groups with unfavorable underlying risk, as they transfer that risk to the health insurance company.

We always look for average renewal increases of around 10 percent or less. To us, this indicates a group with favorable claims experience, and while they may have bad years (everyone does), they are making wise choices and taking care of themselves from an overall risk evaluation perspective. **For most employers, the dynamic is counterintuitive—the best time to transition into a self-insured contract is when an employer receives a low single-digit renewal increase or even a rate hold.** The worst time is when that same employer receives a high renewal increase. There is an old adage, "The best time to fix the roof is when it's sunny outside (low to no renewal increase), not when it's raining (high increase)."

Benefit Education and Communication

Every ideal member of Captivated Health should value communication and education very highly. This means that management communicates benefits and plan details clearly to their people, including every change, addition, or adjustment.

They should also educate their people—building their literacy—about the plan and the available options.

This only works when everyone is on board. The more you pay attention to the quality of healthcare you get and the price you pay for it, the lower your premiums will stay over the long term. That's what your employees really care about. The first thing they look at is how much money their employer takes out of their paycheck through payroll contributions. The second thing they look at is the out-of-pocket exposure they have on any given plan option. They're asking, "If I use my plan, what are going to be my financial responsibilities?"

We want to make sure that the organization is willing to communicate and educate its people in order to keep them informed and empowered by their health plan benefits.

Risk Management

Today's claims are tomorrow's premiums.[IP] Our ideal captive member understands this mantra. They fully acknowledge that health insurance costs are a direct result of the decisions their employees make. **If they really want to change the outcome, they have to manage risk**. They do so by first taking responsibility as fiduciaries, then, second, by looking at the data for information about what needs to be done. Third, they work with their health benefits advisor to select the right solution that actually solves the problem. By doing that, they lower their claims, and when they lower their claims, they save money, and so do their employees.

10

Preparing for Your Health Insurance Hacker Transformation

✳

I F YOU ARE in alignment with the ideal mindsets from the last chapter and score at least 75 percent overall on the Community Assessment, you might be ready to move forward with Captivated Health. If you found a few categories you don't quite align with, use those misalignments as opportunities for improvement. You might be a perfect candidate in the making, but there are a few steps to complete before you're fully ready to make the transition.

Qualitative Preparation

If your issue is with one of the mindsets, we first need to pinpoint where the misalignment is. Is your C-Suite disconnected from the health insurance discussion? That is a relatively simple fix in that it only requires a deliberate choice and a mindset change. If the issue is group size, that's more of an issue that can only be overcome with more growth, and if you reach out to us, we can have a conversation about it and help you figure out the best course of action with an alternate solution like level-funding.

Maybe you're feeling less than confident about healthcare education in your organization. We can certainly help you establish best practices for communication and education to get you exactly where you need to be to join a self-insured captive. It's essential to get your people on board to ensure participation and engagement. In fact, it's the single biggest determinant of success.

If you have questions about how to better prepare for switching to self-insurance, you can find more resources at CaptivatedHealth.com.

Quantitative Preparation

What if you score top marks in all the mindset categories but have a less-than-attractive risk profile? We've got tools for you there, too.

We've put together a Risk Profile Scorecard to help you evaluate how an underwriter would look at the risk of your group. We ask for a ranking between one and four in a variety of areas, including:

- Group Size
- Renewal History
- Plan Participation
- Number of Carriers
- Claims Experience
- Large Claimants

Risk Evaluation

		1	2	3	4	Score
1	Group Size	Fewer than 50 Employees	50 - 75 employees	75 - 99 employees	More than 100 employees	0
2	Renewal History	Over the past 2-3 years, our average health insurance renewal increase has been 20% or more (not including plan changes)	Over the past 2-3 years, our average health insurance renewal increase has been between 15-20% (not including plan changes)	Over the past 2-3 years, our average health insurance renewal increase has been between 10-15% (not including plan changes)	Over the past 2-3 years, our average health insurance renewal increase has been less than 10% (not including plan changes)	0
3	Plan Participation	Less than 50% of eligible employees are enrolled	50% to 74% of eligible employees are enrolled	75% to 90% of eligible employees are enrolled	Over 90% of eligible employees are enrolled	0
4	Number of Carriers	More than 3 carriers in the past 5 years	3 carriers in the past 5 years	2 carriers in the past 5 years	1 carrier in the past 5 years	0
5	Claims Experience	Claims experience is not available	Up to 1 year of claims data is available	1 - 2 years of claims data is available	More than 2 years of claims data is available	0
6	Large Claimants	No large claimant information is available	Up to 1 year of large claimant data is available	1 - 2 years of large claimant data is available	More than 2 years of large claimant data is available	0
	Scorecard					0 / 24, 0%

All of these elements help us to evaluate what level of risk your company brings to the table. A score of 75 percent or higher would indicate that being self-insured would work for your group. If you are interested in completing this scorecard, visit CaptivatedHealth.com/Book or scan the following QR code.

If you score below 75 percent, there are things you can do to improve your risk profile. For example, Medicare is health insurance for Americans who are sixty-five years of age or older. Once you reach that age, you have an opportunity to transition off the company's plan and enroll in Medicare instead. In most cases, Medicare is a better value for the individual as the coverage is comparable and it costs less money.

The law expressly prohibits employers from ending an active employee's coverage when they turn sixty-five, requiring

Medicare enrollment as a condition of employment (for employers with twenty-plus employees), or financially rewarding or openly encouraging anyone who is Medicare-eligible to disenroll from the company plan. Essentially, you can't force them off the plan. Why? Because as we get older, we spend more on healthcare. It's more cost-effective for the government to keep people on their company plan than to allow them to enroll in Medicare.

As an employer, you cannot influence any of your eligible employees to take Medicare, but **you can educate them about their options**. If they are educated about the design of Medicare plans and aware of the potential cost savings, they are more likely to opt in to Medicare of their own volition. This is a service Borislow Insurance provides our clients and one of our most beloved practices.

As a result, your employee usually saves money, and you typically remove some high-cost claim risk from your plan because the likelihood of a sixty-five-year-old having a stroke, heart attack, cancer, or some other major claim is much higher than someone who is twenty-five. This strategy improves the value of the benefit for your eligible employees and improves your risk profile at the same time.

Another way to get your risk profile in the right place is to utilize a **Health Savings Account** structured plan, also known as a Consumer-Driven Health Plan (CDHP). As I mentioned before, we have a track record of helping employers achieve a 26 percent enrollment rate in the first year of offering an HSA. We've helped some organizations achieve complete enrollment within only three years.

This can be the best method for getting your people on the same side of the cost equation as you are when you switch your health insurance plan financing to self-funding. Once your employees have HSAs, and you fund those accounts at

50 percent of the health plan deductible for your employees to use on their healthcare, you're now giving them a portion of the money you used to pay an insurance company (premium). If they are smarter about the way they access healthcare and don't spend all of it, they get to keep it in their account and it rolls forward to the next year, where it earns interest. If they invest it in a mutual fund, they begin compounding that money over time, which will include annual contributions you make each plan year. One added feature is your employees can put their own money in as well, up to the annual IRS limits, and best of all, every dollar invested is tax-preferred.

We like to call it the triple crown of taxes: money goes in tax-preferred, it grows with no tax, and as long as you spend it on qualified medical expenses (IRS code Section 213d), you'll never pay a dime of tax on any distributions. You also have the freedom to spend that money on other expenses like a TV, vacation, or new car, but doing so will trigger a taxable event for the HSA account owner with a 20 percent penalty plus applicable income tax if withdrawn before the age of sixty-five, and only income tax post sixty-five. It's the **only account structure of its kind in the IRS code.**

When your employees all get engaged, you're paying them to do the things they already know they should be doing. Everyone knows they should have a primary care doctor to maintain their health. They know they should look for generic drug alternatives when they take a prescription drug. As the money builds up year after year, they have the resources they need to fund medical expenses in their retirement. This is another way you can get your employees to start caring about the decisions they make by painting the long-term need to save.

As I said earlier in the book, if people have the same co-pay no matter what decision they make, they will care less about cost, which increases cost to the plan, primarily funded by you as their employer. Conversely, when they have an incentive to make smarter choices, everyone is rowing in the same direction. You reduce your health plan risk by creating health-smart, financially conscious participants in your plan.

All of these concepts are encapsulated in *Bend the Healthcare Trend,* which is a companion book to Captivated Health. Implemented together, engaging your employees through CDHP/HSAs and then changing the way you finance your health insurance creates a win-win-win.

Advanced Concepts and Solutions

Once you successfully transition into a self-insured captive, you and your employees are comfortably operating on the platform, and you, as the plan sponsor, are receiving health plan data, the world of opportunity opens up for you to make a difference.

Earlier, we shared some stories of creative solutions our clients have implemented as a result of that data and the insight it provides. Now let's dig a little deeper and discuss other, more advanced concepts and solutions you might consider to improve quality and lower cost.

Pharmacy Benefits

PBMs control the supply and cost of medications for your people, which are growing exponentially in cost. Historically, pharmacy claims were 15 percent of the total cost of health insurance. Today, that percentage is 25 percent and growing faster than any other component. What can you do about it? When your organization is self-insured, you can "carve out" your PBM, negotiate a transparent contract with no spread pricing, and, most importantly, gain access to the pharmacy rebates associated with the drugs your people are taking. In many cases, those rebates are thousands of dollars.

When you are fully-insured, you can't carve this benefit out of the plan, and by leaving it in the control of the health insurance carrier, they get to keep your pharmacy rebates. In Captivated Health, we help you take control of this element of your health insurance plan, and you get to receive those quarterly rebates, helping you build your reserves.

One client story to help this opportunity hit home is from a conversation I had with the CFO of a very small (50 employees) independent school in Maine. When the first rebate check was delivered, he called me and said, "Mark, I got my first pharmacy rebate check today for $38,000. Do you know what that means to me?"

I responded, "$38,000?"

He laughed and said, "Yes, and that is the cost of a full-time staff member for my school. I don't like the fact that my people are taking all this medication, but they are, and before we joined Captivated Health, the insurance company was keeping that money. Now we get to keep it."

I said, "Yes, and you will get another check in the same amount next quarter and the quarter after that as long as your people keep taking those drugs." In essence, the pharmacy rebates lower the cost of his overall health claims. It's an offset and financial recovery.

Primary Care

Primary care refers to the first point of contact people have with the healthcare system. It is the foundation of health services and emphasizes comprehensive, accessible, continuous, and coordinated care for individuals across all ages, backgrounds, and health needs.

It is the ongoing, whole-person healthcare that keeps people healthy, manages everyday medical needs, and coordinates specialized care when necessary. On average, about five to seven cents of every premium dollar in the fully-insured market is invested in primary care, which underscores one of the persistent challenges in the healthcare system. **Primary care is underfunded**, even though it's foundational for prevention, continuity, and coordination of care. Many experts argue that investing in primary care can improve outcomes and reduce overall costs.[10]

There are three forms of primary care in our healthcare system: traditional primary care, concierge primary care, and direct primary care. Below is a chart highlighting the differences.

	Direct Primary Care	Concierge Medicine	Traditional Primary Care
	Patients typically pay a flat membership fee of about $100/month for unlimited access to a physician.	Patients pay for care on a fee-for-service basis. Patients also pay an additional flat fee for priority access to a primary care physician.	Patients pay for care on a fee-for-service basis.
Convenience	Call, text, email, video chat or visit provider just about any time.	Call or email for appointment. Annual fee buys quicker access to doctor.	Call or email for appointment.
Patient Experience	Build a personal relationship with a provider. Patient is the client.	Build a personal relationship with a provider, who can serve as an advocate for patient before specialists and rest of healthcare system.	Depending on size of the practice, patient may see one doctor or a different doctor each time. Insurer pays, so patients may need to dispute denied claims.
Access to care	Unlimited access to physician can result in fewer emergency room visits, earlier screenings and improved chronic disease management.	Annual fee covers screening and tests not typically covered by insurance. Patients must get referrals for diagnostic work or specialist care.	Patients must typically get referrals for diagnostic work or specialist care.
Insurance	Providers generally do not accepte insurance. Health plans may not accept referrals to specialists from direct primary care physicians.	Patient generally responsible for co-pays and cost-sharing for additional services. Concierge physicians generally belong to insurance networks, so they can refer patients to in-network specialists.	Patient generally responsible co-pays for office visits and cost-sharing for additional services.
Healthcare Accounts		HSA, HRA, FSA	HSA, HRA, FSA
Cost	Monthly membership fee is separate from insurance plan and does not count toward deductible. Patients may have to pay for diagnostics and other uncovered services. Direct primary care practices typically negotiate preferred cash prices with external providers for patients.	Annual fees do not count toward health plan deductible. Co-pays and out-of-pocket costs do.	Co-pays typically do not count toward deductible, but out-of-pocket expenditures do.

Captivated Health

---

[10]   "Implementing High-Quality Primary Care: Rebuilding the Foundation of Health Care." *National Academies of Sciences, Engineering, and Medicine.* 2021. Washington, DC: The National Academies Press. https://doi.org/10.17226/25983. Accessed August 25, 2025.

The biggest difference is the alignment of interests for the consumer. In a nutshell, traditional and concierge primary care accept a fee for service (paid by the health insurance company) for the care they deliver, and in many cases, those primary care doctors' practices are owned by a major hospital system. Why is that important? Each of those practices represents about $2 million of referral revenue to the hospital system, aligning their interests with the system rather than the consumer.

Direct primary care (DPC) is different. It's a return to a TV show in the 1970s called *Marcus Welby, M.D.*, where the main character focused on a dedication to his patients, often making house calls and emphasizing a personal, hands-on approach to medicine. DPC is a membership-based model of healthcare delivery where people (or their employers) pay doctors directly, usually through a flat monthly or annual fee, instead of going through traditional health insurance billing. This construct aligns the interests of the primary doctor with the consumer rather than the system.

DPC doctors often manage a smaller list of people (500 to 800, rather than 2,000-plus), allowing more time for each visit and interaction. Pricing is transparent, predictable, and with fewer surprise medical bills. In short, **DPC is like a subscription-based gym membership but for your doctor**. You pay a predictable monthly fee for easy, ongoing access to primary care, and because of the newly enacted One Big Beautiful Bill, DPC fees can now be paid for through a Health Savings Account, as it has been reclassified in the IRS code as a 213d eligible medical expense—a major shift in public policy.

Why is this an important concept for a self-insured captive plan sponsor? Offering and paying for a DPC benefit for employees (and families) will reduce healthcare claims for the plan sponsor and out-of-pocket expenses for the plan participant. More importantly, it will help your people improve their health and avoid more expensive forms of healthcare because it focuses on prevention and well-being.

Direct Contracting

Most employers are familiar and comfortable with using one of the BUCA provider networks because it is what they have always known. Brand identity and trust cloud the enormous amount of money spent by employers on accessing those networks they offer. Most employers are unaware of the network access fees that are included in their administrative portion of the premiums they are paying, and in many cases, those fees are twenty to twenty-five dollars per employee per month, which is only the cost for access, not the actual care provided. Carriers will argue those fees are necessary to maintain the network, credential providers, and manage care.

Direct contracting in healthcare is a provider access model that bypasses insurance companies by contracting directly with healthcare providers (usually hospital systems or large physician groups) to deliver care for the plan participants (e.g., surgeries, maternity care, chronic condition management, centers of excellence).

The key features of this strategy:

1. Direct relationship with the providers of healthcare, where payment terms are negotiated directly with the providers without going through an insurance carrier as the middleman.

2. Custom agreements or contracts that often are structured as bundled payments, capitation rates, or discounted fee schedules tailored to the population's needs.

3. Cost control that removes administrative layers, reduces insurance overhead, and allows more transparency in pricing.

4. Quality focus, which is built into the contracts and may include performance guarantees, quality metrics, or outcome-based incentives (e.g., fewer hospital readmissions).

5. Employee experience, which often includes enhanced access to care, such as centers of excellence, on-site or near-site clinics, or streamlined referral agreements.

The Harpeth Hall School case study, shared in Chapter One, is a classic example of direct contracting, highlighting its benefit to the plan participant and the plan sponsor. Direct contracting lowers large claim costs, improves outcomes on high-cost procedures, and enhances the transparency of hospital pricing.

These three advanced concepts and strategies can be implemented when the employer enters into the self-insured captive model (aggressive) or in future years to bolster the performance of the plan (more commonplace).

In short, taking control of your pharmacy expenses is possible when you carve out your PBM. DPC keeps your people healthy and out of the hospital, while direct contracting ensures the hospital care they do need is high-quality and reasonably priced.

Together, these three strategies form a sustainable self-funded model that gives employers cost control and employees a better experience.

**DIRECT PRIMARY CARE + PBM CARVEOUT +
DIRECT CONTRACTING**

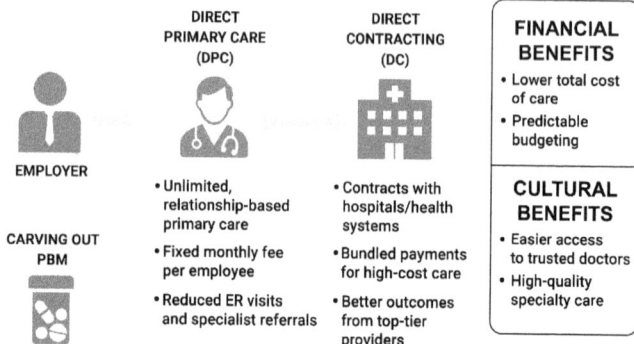

Captivated Health

Next Steps

Finally, maybe the most important thing you can do to prepare for transitioning to a self-funded plan is to start working with us. And yes, that would mean you have to stop working with your current broker. If you're fed up with the fully-insured hamster wheel of less bad renewals, if you want to bring greater value to your people and their health and well-being, if you want to significantly lower your health insurance costs, and if you're serious about taking control of your own organization's health, then it's time to take the first step.

We care deeply about restoring confidence in health insurance and benefits, making sure your people get the help, support, and care they deserve, and giving you and them the tools to win in the healthcare casino. We're here to help whenever you are ready. The journey to an empowered health insurance future starts with one step.

Acknowledgments

TO MY WIFE, Eleonora Cino, my second chance at love. You are my peace and the person who accepts all of me and brings out the very best in me. This book would not be possible without your encouragement to write it—and for the first time, "go it alone" publishing a book. I am grateful God sent you into my life, and I'm excited about the future, one where we both grow individually and together and help each other reach for our biggest dreams and aspirations—like Tranquillo Solutions, LLC, your new platform to help entrepreneurs activate their visions. Both of us share a passion to make a difference, and this book is a wonderful example of that commitment. You are a beautiful human being—I am fortunate to have you as my life partner.

To my amazing kids, Grayson, Kelly, and Brooke. Each one of you is special to me, and I am proud to see the lives you are building as young entrepreneurs in this challenging and equally exciting world. You are all strong, smart, resilient, hard-working, and caring about the people you love—and each one of you has big dreams for your life that I will do what I can to support you to realize. My goal as your dad has always been to love you, teach you, and encourage you to pursue your passions and live a life of meaning. You are all on that path, and I appreciate all the experiences and memories we are creating together.

To my business partner, Jennifer Borislow, who, twenty-one years ago, invited me to be her business partner in Borislow Insurance and transform a successful local business she founded into a national employee benefits and brokerage firm. Together, we created a team of almost one hundred benefit superheroes who are passionate about making a difference in our clients' lives by leveraging and collaborating on their unique abilities. BI is the foundation that sets the stage for our team to create the Captivated Health Platform to serve our clients. I will always be grateful to you for believing and investing in me—and proud of the return I have generated for you, our team, clients, and strategic partners on that investment. Our story is remarkable.

To the original ten private, independent school founders in New Hampshire and Maine—most notably Jill Duncan, retired CFO at New Hampton School, and John Ferris, retired CFO at Proctor Academy, who were the first schools to join Captivated Health for Education on July 1, 2014, and their schools remain on the platform eleven-plus years later. Your shared passion and support of our vision to solve the health insurance challenge for private schools is how this platform was created, and I will be forever grateful to you for collaborating with us and for getting eight of your peers to join in the beginning. Today, Captivated Health Education serves almost thirty private schools in seven states and is growing in select markets across the country, helping schools accumulate over $40 million on their collective balance sheets. Your belief in us and commitment to a bigger, better health insurance future are missed and will always be remembered. You are both unforgettable, and this is part of your legacy.

And finally, to the team at BI and Captivated Health, whom it would be hard to name individually, having you in our company is what makes us unique in the market. Your individual super-powers coming together for the collective is what makes us special. Thank you for being mission-driven, creating value for each other and for our clients, and for sharing a passion to make a difference. Together, we are positively impacting lives by making healthcare and benefits easier and more affordable for people. It is a noble mission.

About the Author

MARK S. GAUNYA is a principal at Borislow Insurance and the Founder of Captivated Health, located in Boston, Massachusetts. He is an employee benefits advisor with over three decades of experience and a tireless, passionate advocate for transparency, consumerism, health, and well-being. He is a pioneer in the use of Consumer-Driven Health and Wellness Plans (CDHP) to lower healthcare costs and improve overall health, which is the genesis of *Bend the Healthcare Trend*, a book he co-authored in 2009, with the second edition released in 2017.

Mark was named as a national Top 30 Benefits Advisor to Watch by Employee Benefit News and Employee Benefit Adviser and was awarded Most Innovative Broker of the Year. In 2024 and 2025, the Captivated Health® platform earned recognition by Berkley Accident & Health for Excellence in Health Risk Management.

Mark was an eight-year Member of the Board of Directors for the Massachusetts Health Connector, a past National Legislative Council Chair for the National Association of Benefits & Insurance Professionals (NABIP), and the co-creator of the NABIP Healthcare Consumer Bill of Rights.

Mark earned his GBA from Wharton, and he is certified in the ACA and Self-funding by NABIP.

Mark is a graduate of the University of Rhode Island and resides in Hopkinton, MA.

Captivated Health®
the greatest wealth is health

CONTROL YOUR HEALTH INSURANCE COSTS

Change Your Financing To Change Your Future.

CaptivatedHealth.com

THIS BOOK IS PROTECTED INTELLECTUAL PROPERTY

Instant IP [IP]

The author of this book values Intellectual Property. The book you just read is protected by Instant IP[IP], a proprietary process, which integrates blockchain technology giving Intellectual Property "Global Protection." By creating a "Time-Stamped" smart contract that can never be tampered with or changed, we establish "First Use" that tracks back to the author.

Instant IP [IP] functions much like a Pre-Patent since it provides an immutable "First Use" of the Intellectual Property. This is achieved through our proprietary process of leveraging blockchain technology and smart contracts. As a result, proving "First Use" is simple through a global and verifiable smart contract. By protecting intellectual property with blockchain technology and smart contracts, we establish a "First to File" event.

Protected by Instant IP [IP]

LEARN MORE AT INSTANTIP.TODAY